the simple guide to BIRD CARE & Training

by Julie Rach

T.F.H. Publications, Inc.

D1402797

© 2002 T.F.H. Publications, Inc.

Distributed in the UNITED STATES to the Pet Trade by T.F.H. Publications, Inc., 1 TFH Plaza, Neptune City, NJ 07753; on the Internet at www.tfh.com; in CANADA by Rolf C. Hagen Inc., 3225 Sartelon St., Montreal, Quebec H4R 1E8; Pet Trade by H & L Pet Supplies Inc., 27 Kingston Crescent, Kitchener, Ontario N2B 2T6; in ENGLAND by T.F.H. Publications, PO Box 74, Havant PO9 5TT; in AUSTRALIA AND THE SOUTH PACIFIC by T.F.H. (Australia), Pty. Ltd., Box 149, Brookvale 2100 N.S.W., Australia; in NEW ZEALAND by Brooklands Aquarium Ltd., 5 McGiven Drive, New Plymouth, RD1 New Zealand; in SOUTH AFRICA by Rolf C. Hagen S.A. (PTY.) LTD., P.O. Box 201199, Durban North 4016, South Africa; in Japan by T.F.H. Publications. Published by T.F.H. Publications, Inc.

Printed and bound in China by T.F.H. Publications, Inc.

Contents

"Birds for Beginners" page 20

"Bird Proofing" page 77

"Tips to Teach Talking" page 190

Part One
Bringing a Bird Into Your Life

"Sir, Before I hand over the canary, I'm afraid I have to question Your motives for wanting a bird."

Starting Out

Congratulations on your decision to add a pet bird to your home and life. Adopting a pet bird is a big commitment. It will require time, energy, and money on your part. In many ways, the commitment to bird ownership resembles parenthood. This small, cute, reasonably helpless creature will depend on you for its every need. Unlike a child, though, your pet will never "leave the nest." You will be responsible for its care and entertainment for the rest of its life. In some species of pet birds, this means a life span that mirrors our own.

Before you think this bird-owner relationship only benefits the bird, think again. With a bird in your life, you'll never again come home to an empty house. You won't have to wonder what to do for

Are you ready to share your life with a bird?

Think Ahead

Bird ownership is a lifelong commitment. Think carefully before buying a pet—there are already too many abandoned or neglected birds in the world.

entertainment when nothing's on television, and you'll probably begin to eat better, too, because you'll have so many tempting fresh fruits and vegetables in your refrigerator to feed your pet.

But I'm getting ahead of myself. Let's get back to that "big commitment" I mentioned. Are you sure you're ready for bird ownership? Long before you get one, you'll need to do some serious thinking about whether or not you're ready and willing to bring a bird into your home. Take as long as you need to determine if a bird will fit into your life because there's a saying that goes, "Most cats have nine lives, but most parrots have nine homes." Ideally, bird ownership is a lifelong commitment, but many birds are rehomed several times during their lifetimes because owners didn't think through their commitment before the bird came into their homes.

If possible, "borrow" someone else's pet bird to give bird ownership a trial run. Perhaps you have bird-owning friends who need someone to watch their pet while they're on vacation. Real-life experience can help you decide if bird ownership is for you.

I was lucky enough to be able to bird-sit for a flock of five parrots that were pets of some dear friends. I took care of these birds for about ten days and had a chance to experience the pros and the cons of bird ownership. I decided that the noise and the mess were worth the effort, and I enjoyed the antics and interactions of the different birds. I also took care of two other birds for a co-worker while she and her husband were out of town. On one occasion, she brought them to the office and I cared for them there, while at other times, I took care of the birds in their home. I'd stop by to feed and water them on my way to work, then visit them again for a more extended period after work. During the evening visit, the birds were allowed to come out of their cages for scratching and cuddling if they were up to it. After I got my own bird, a troubled African grey, I continued to be a bird-sitter for both sets of friends.

In my case, I had about six months to consider my African grey's adoption. A friend first discussed the idea of me adopting the grey in the fall of 1988, and it was the spring of 1989 before her previous owners were really willing to give her up. During the time between the initial offer and her arrival, I thought long and hard about what it would mean to have this creature in my home. I checked with my landlord to find out if pet birds were permitted, I considered where her cage would go in my apartment, I scouted out pet stores to determine which ones sold quality bird products, and I inquired about avian veterinarians in my area. I learned as much as I could about the African grey's temperament and its dietary needs. I also found out as much as I could about the bird's personality and pet qualities. Because my bird had a variety of physical and emotional problems, I wanted to be sure I was ready to take her in and give her the care and attention she deserved. I think my planning prior to her arrival helped ease her transition into my home, and knowing where the veterinary clinic and pet store were before I had a medical emergency or sudden shortage of a favorite treat helped me settle into bird ownership more comfortably.

Consider hands-on research when making a choice.

You'll need to look at your lifestyle to see if a bird will fit into it well, and you'll need to discuss your plans with family members or roommates because their lives will be affected by the bird's presence in your home.

Questions To Answer

Read over and answer the following questions about bird ownership to further determine whether or not you're prepared to add a feathered friend to your home:

How much money do you have in your budget for bird care?

How much time do you have in your schedule to care for a bird?

How much time do you think bird care takes each day?

How much time do you spend away from home each day?

How many children are in your home?

How many other pets do you have?

Will someone be able to take care of your bird if you go on vacation?

Are there any noise restrictions on your home?

Are there any pet restrictions on your home?

Are you comfortable handling a bird?

Have you owned birds before?

Do you have allergies?

Is your home filled with antiques or other valuable décor?

Are you a neat freak?

Will a birdcage and a playgym fit in your home?

Why do you want a bird? There are no "right" or "wrong" answers to these questions—answer them as honestly as you can based on your situation. These questions are simply designed to make you consider some of the day-to-day requirements of a pet bird, as well as some of the personality quirks that new bird owners don't always consider before they adopt their new pet.

Birds cost money, even if you receive them for free. My African grey, which was a "free bird," cost me about $2,000 a year to feed, care for, entertain, and occasionally board at my veterinarian's office when I went out of town. Her annual cost of care was higher than normal because she had a number of long-standing medical conditions that required routine medication and sometimes hospitalization.

Be certain you have room for new housemates.

When deciding what type of bird you want, look at your budget and be realistic about what you can afford. Although it's tempting to purchase the most expensive parrot in the bird store, please don't do it. Remember that the money in your budget needs to cover not only the cost of the bird, but also the cost of bringing it home and setting up its home. Take note of the price of a suitable cage and other accessories, as well as food, when you shop for your pet bird. Also make sure you have money in your budget for an initial veterinary examination and routine procedures, such as nail trimming and wing clipping, that your bird will require.

Each day birds need to have their cages cleaned and their meals prepared. They also need to interact with their owners because they are naturally social "flock" animals. Birds can fit into homes that have children and other pets in them, but it requires a little planning and organization on the bird owner's part to make it work. Birds have homes and other accessories, such as playgyms, that need to fit comfortably into your home in order to keep them safe and content. You also need to be satisfied with the size and placement of these items in your home or else the bird-owner relationship will be problematic from the start. To make sure your bird's paraphernalia fits in your home, measure the base of the cage and the playgym at the pet store, then draw a cardboard or paper template of the dimensions. Place the template in different parts of your home until you find a spot that will accommodate the cage and the playgym. Make sure that these locations are not in some out-of-the-way, little-used guest room, basement, or attic. Your bird needs to feel like it's part of the family, so putting its cage in the family room, living room, or dining room will help bring it into family activities.

Be aware that birds are sometimes noisy, often messy, and can be intimidating to handle, especially if you've never done it before. Some species–cockatoos, cockatiels, and African greys, in particular–can also cause allergic reactions in sensitive people. This is because these species have powder down on their feathers that creates dust as the bird preens.

> **Think Ahead**
> Your budget needs to be able to handle not only the cost of the bird, but the initial cost of housing and supplies.

> **The Time Factor**
> One thing potential bird owners need to consider before adopting a pet bird is the amount of time bird care takes every day. I mention this not to put people off bird-keeping, but rather to give future bird owners a realistic appreciation of what's required of them.

A very cute baby hawk-headed parrot.

A single pet bird will need at least 30 minutes in the morning and in the evening for meal preparation. Add to that at least 30 more minutes in the morning for the bird to have time out of its cage for exercise and playtime. If you are lucky enough to work at home, you can adjust your schedule and your bird's cage or playgym location to make the most of your time together. In the evening, your bird will need at least another 30 to 45 minutes of play and cuddle time outside its cage with you. In addition, you will need to devote about 15 minutes each day to changing the water and food bowls in the cage and changing the paper in the cage tray. Each week, you'll need to devote 30 minutes to an hour to cage scrubbing and disinfecting (the amount of time required depends on the size of your bird's cage and the amount of accessories it has in the cage). If you have more than one pet bird, you'll need to adjust your schedule accordingly.

Where Will You Get Your Bird?

Bird owners can find their new pets at pet or bird specialty stores, from breeders, from bird rescue groups, at bird marts or through classified advertisements. Some sources are better

What Do You Want From A Bird?

Characteristic	Steer Toward	Steer Away From
Cuddler	Cockatoo	Amazon or Canary
Showoff	Amazon or Macaw	African grey
Talker	African grey or Parakeet	Cockatoo or Finch
Trickster	Cockatoo, Macaw, or Amazon	Pionus
High-energy pet	Caique or Quaker	Cockatoo or Macaw
Quieter pet	Pionus	

than others for first-time bird owners, so let's consider each a bit more carefully.

Pet stores or bird specialty stores are often the best place for a new bird owner to acquire his or her pet. Not only do many of these stores offer a wide variety of birds and the supplies needed to keep them, but the store's staff can be a great resource for questions and information. They can refer new bird owners to bird clubs, avian veterinarians, and bird rescue groups in an area.

> **Where To Get Your Bird**
>
> Animal Shelter
> Bird Mart
> Bird Rescue Group
> Breeder
> Pet Store
> Private Home

Breeders are another good resource for first-time bird owners. Some bird breeders sell directly to the public, while others market their birds through local pet or bird specialty stores. In addition to young birds, breeders will occasionally offer adult birds for sale that are past their breeding prime but that may make suitable pets in the right home.

Bird rescue groups frequently have a wide variety of birds available for adoption. Some require that potential owners attend orientation sessions to learn about the responsibilities of bird ownership, while others have different screening processes in place for potential owners. In addition to providing birds with homes, the staffs of such groups may also be able to provide referrals to avian veterinarians and bird care information to new owners. Contact rescue groups in your area to find out if they have birds available that are suitable for first-time owners.

Curtains have great appeal for birds on the loose.

Animal shelters sometimes end up with "found" birds or birds that have to be placed in new homes for various reasons. Although you aren't as likely to find a parrot at your animal shelter as you might a dog or a cat, you may want to contact the shelter to inquire if they ever take in homeless birds.

A singing canary adds life to any room.

Bird marts may or may not be good places for first-time owners to purchase birds. Although many marts offer on-site veterinary examinations, the setup of the mart (usually a day-long or weekend-long event at a fairground or auditorium) offers little recourse to owners whose birds develop health or behavioral problems after the mart has concluded. Bird marts do offer bird shoppers a chance to see a wide variety of different species in the same place, so they may be useful when trying to determine which type of bird is best for you. Breeders are available to answer questions, and books, magazines, and videos are offered for sale during these marts.

Bird marts also offer bird owners, especially those with more than one pet, an opportunity to shop for a variety of bird-care supplies in one location. If your area does not have a pet supply superstore or large bird specialty store, a bird mart may be the best outlet for you to purchase bird supplies at economical prices.

Classified advertisements may be the least useful place for a first-time owner to purchase a bird. As in the case of bird marts, there's little follow-up information to someone answering a classified advertisement. Many birds offered for sale through these ads are healthy birds that make suitable pets, but some may have health or behavioral problems that would make them unsuitable. Ask yourself, "Why would someone give up a healthy, happy bird?" when reading these ads and remember the old saying "Buyer beware" before purchasing a bird through such an advertisement.

Sometimes birds just find you. One of my fellow editors on *Bird Talk* magazine first became interested in keeping birds after she rescued a cockatiel from her backyard swimming pool. In another case, a different editor also ended up with a cockatiel after neighborhood children brought one to his door because his house "had a lot of birds in it, so you'll know what to do."

My story is also like that–a series of seemingly unrelated incidents that occurred over a period of about 18 months and that ended happily for my parrot and me. When her

Questions to Ask When Purchasing a Bird From a Private Party:

How long have you had the bird?

Where did the bird come from before you owned it?

Has the bird been seen by an avian veterinarian recently? If so, does it have any health problems I should know about?

Why are you selling the bird?

What does the bird eat?

What's its normal activity level like?

Does it have any unusual behaviors I should know about?

Questions to Ask When Purchasing a Bird From a Store or Breeder:

How long have you had the bird?

Where did the bird come from before you owned it?

What does the bird eat?

What's its normal activity level like?

Has the bird been seen by an avian veterinarian recently? If so, does it have any health problems I should know about?

Does it have any unusual behaviors I should know about?

Do you offer a health guarantee with the bird?

Can I call you with follow-up questions after I purchase the bird?

previous owners first planned to find her a new home, a different woman in the office who also loved African greys was going to be her owner. However, my bird's owners decided to keep her a while longer, claiming that they couldn't bear to part with her. In the meantime, the other African grey lover took a job with another company and left the office. Because she owned several other African greys at the time, my parrot's physical and emotional problems might have ended up being more of a burden than a joy for her. As a dear friend of mine often reminds me, "everything worked out the way it was supposed to," because my bird got to be a well-loved only pet of an owner who had the resources to give her the care and attention she needed.

Hand-Feeding: To Finish or Not To Finish?

I am not known for sharing my opinions at large on many subjects. When I worked at *Bird Talk,* my oft-quoted line at pet trade shows was "I don't have opinions because it makes my life so much easier." I do have opinions, but I usually keep them to myself, especially in situations like trade shows where I'm representing the company I work for.

Hand-feeding is best left to the experts.

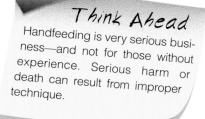

Think Ahead

Handfeeding is very serious business—and not for those without experience. Serious harm or death can result from improper technique.

I'm going to break with my usual keep-my-opinions-to-myself method because this next opinion is important–it may be life-or-death important for a chick out there, so please pay attention: *Only highly experienced breeders and bird owners should finish hand-feeding a bird. This is not a job for novices.*

In earlier bird-care books, many experts (including me) said that it was important to bond with your young bird, and the best bonds were built during the hand-feeding and weaning processes. Since expressing this opinion, I have watched several friends–level-headed, caring, intelligent, professional people who do not rattle easily or become discouraged quickly–suffer through the hand-feeding and weaning of their parrots. The frustration these people went through really did not help them build better relationships with their birds. In fact, I'm surprised they chose to stick with bird-keeping because the process was such an ordeal. Your chick will develop a healthy, normal relationship with you if it is already weaned when you get it, and you'll enjoy bird-keeping much more right from the start if your pet is already eating "normal" food when you bring it home.

Is a Young or a Mature Bird Right for Me?

When shopping for your pet, you may find adult birds offered for sale in addition to the current crop of young birds. Be sure to determine the reasons for an

Clear eyes are a key indicator of good health.

Top Ten Beginning Parrots

Brotogeris: The active nature and mild temperament of these parrots makes them a good choice for first-time owners.

Parakeet: Parakeets are the perennial "first bird" because of their widespread availability, small size, mellow temperament, quiet voices, and affordable price.

Cockatiel: Second in popularity to the parakeet, cockatiels offer many of the attractive qualities of a cockatoo—the colorful crest, the elegant look, and the curious nature—in a much more manageable size for first-time owners. Also, the cockatiel's voice is easier on the ear than the cockatoo's, and the cockatiel isn't as emotionally needy as its larger cousin. Finally, the cockatiel's take-home price tag won't break the bank like a cockatoo's can.

Conure: With their wide range of colors and sizes, conures offer something for every bird owner. Whether you want a talker, a trickster, or a cuddler, a conure is for you! Many conures are just the right size for first-time owners to handle, and their clever natures make them irresistible.

Lovebird: Who couldn't love a lovebird? These pint-sized, colorful parrots pack a lot of personality and charm into their tiny bodies, and they're an entertaining and affordable way to get into the hobby of bird-keeping.

Parrotlet: Although not as flashy as a lovebird on the outside, a parrotlet has just as much personality on the inside. These bold, saucy little birds quickly capture their owners' hearts and are soon ruling the roost in their homes.

Pionus: First-time bird owners who want to start with a "big bird" can't go wrong with a pionus. These parrots are ideal for either an apartment or a single-family home because of their quiet natures. They are also mellow enough to blend into a family setting.

Psittacula: The bright colors and elegant plumage of the Psittacula family will catch the eye of any bird lover. These slender parakeets are noted for their speech quality as well as their ability to learn tricks. Psittacula have no problem being the life of the party, which is another aspect of their popularity among bird owners.

Quaker: Quakers have a devoted following in the bird world because of their clever personalities and their abilities to learn to speak and to do tricks. All this talent is available in a medium-size parrot, which is ideal for a first-time owner to handle. Unfortunately, Quakers do not have a devoted following in the world of politics because many states have restrictions on owning these personable little parrots. Make sure Quakers are legal in your state before you bring one home.

Senegal: Senegals are small, brightly colored parrots that quickly become devoted to their owners. They fit right into any home situation, and their outgoing personalities make them a favorite with bird-keepers.

adult bird being placed in a new home before purchasing one. Many good reasons exist for adopting out an adult bird, but sometimes people are simply passing along a bird with behavioral or physical problems that a first-time bird owner may not be ready to handle effectively.

Other Birds for Beginners

Although most people think of parakeets and cockatiels as good "starter pets" for first-time bird owners, canaries and some species of finches can also be suitable pets for new bird owners. They are particularly good pets for owners who want to appreciate their pets' singing ability or active antics inside a spacious cage or indoor aviary.

Those bird owners seeking interactive pets may be better off selecting a member of the parrot family because most canaries and finches aren't as naturally inclined to come out of their cages for playtime and cuddling as many parrots are. However, there are exceptions to every rule, so you'll have to see how your pet reacts if you want to take it out of its cage. Be sure all windows and doors are closed securely before letting your canary or finch out of its cage. As a rule, canaries and finches don't have their wings trimmed as parrots do, but ask your avian veterinarian's opinion on whether or not your canary or finch is a good candidate for wing trimming if it will be spending long periods of time out of its cage under your supervision.

Ask your bird store staff for recommendations on which types of canaries are most likely to sing, and which finch species are suited for first-time bird owners.

Young cockatiels look to their parents for guidance.

Birds in the Wild

As a pet bird owner, it may help you better understand your pet if you know a little bit about how birds live in the wild. Wild parrots are found primarily in tropical and subtropical forests of the Southern Hemisphere. They are found as far north as Afghanistan and as far south as Antipodes Island in New Zealand. More than 200 species are found in Central and South American rainforests, and another 100 live in the South Pacific; 34 species are found in Africa, India, and Southeast Asia. Parrots live in habitats as diverse as the cloud forests of New Guinea, the highlands of Ethiopia, the shoreline and arid interior of Australia, and the southern Alps of New Zealand.

According to the fossil record, parrots have been around for about 30 million years. A leg bone discovered in France from a bird named *Archaeopsittacus verreauxi* and a 20-

Where the Birds Are

Australian ornithologist Joseph Forshaw provides the following regional breakdown of parrot species in his book, *Parrots of the World:*

Brazil	70 species	Trinidad	8 species
Australia	52 species	Myanmar	7 species
Colombia	49 species	Thailand	6 species
Venezuela	48 species	The Malay Peninsula	6 species
New Guinea	46 species	Uruguay	6 species
Indonesia	45 species	Sri Lanka	5 species
Peru	41 species	Indochina	5 species
Ecuador	38 species	Fiji	5 species
Bolivia	38 species	New Caledonia	4 species
The Guianas	29 species	Jamaica	4 species
Argentina	25 species	Puerto Rico	4 species
Panama	20 species	Chile	4 species
Mexico	18 species	Madagascar	3 species
Paraguay	17 species	Comoros	3 species
Costa Rica	16 species	The Mascarene Islands	3 species
Central Africa	14 species	Afghanistan	3 species
Honduras	13 species	China	3 species
Guatemala	12 species	Seychelles	2 species
The Philippines	11 species	Cuba	2 species
The Solomon Islands	11 species	Hispaniola	2 species
Southern Africa	10 species	Iraq	1 species
India	10 species	Iran	1 species
New Zealand	9 species	Tibet	1 species
Northern Africa	8 species		

The Congo African grey, now bred in captivity as pets.

million-year-old fossil of the *Conuropsis* genus found in Nebraska indicate that the ancestors of today's parrots were around millions of years ago. Parrot fossils have also been found in Australia, Africa, and South America.

Finches and canaries, which come from Asia, Africa, Australia, and the Canary Islands, are small active birds. These creatures are colorful and entertaining, with a long history of being kept as pets. They are more social with each other than with humans, so don't expect the same type of companionship you'll get from parrots.

Until the early 20th century, wild parrots could also be found in the continental United States. The Carolina parakeet and the thick-billed parrot had well-established native flocks in the eastern and southwestern United States.

When the first European settlers came to America, Carolina parakeets were widely seen east of the Great Plains from Wisconsin to Louisiana and Florida. Flocks of more than 300 birds were common sights, and a future without these small green-and-yellow parakeets must have seemed unlikely. However, as settlements grew, the parakeets' population declined until their habitat was limited to the Florida swamps and the Mississippi Basin.

The birds' ability to decimate farmland crops worked against them. Rather than eating their traditional diet of cockleburs and native tree seeds, they instead ate settlers' crops, which caused farmers to hunt them as agricultural pests.

Other factors contributing to the demise of the Carolina parakeet included a demand for both the birds' feathers and the birds themselves as decoration for ladies' hats and the fact that Carolina parakeets were considered to be good eating. Hunting of the birds for food and decoration, along with their status as a pest species, sealed their fate around the turn of the century. Their extinction was predicted by ornithologists as early as 1874, and last-ditch preservation efforts were begun shortly thereafter.

In the 1880s, 16 Carolina parakeets were sent to the Cincinnati Zoo, but the birds did not reproduce well in captivity. Perhaps the birds were too old, or perhaps the environment was not to their liking to ensure reproductive success.

By the early 1900s, the zoo was down to a single pair of birds: a female named Lady Jane and a male named Incas. (Coincidentally, Lady Jane and Incas shared an aviary with another representative of a doomed species: Martha, the last passenger pigeon, who died in 1914.) After 32 years in captivity, Lady Jane died in 1917 and Incas died in 1918, at which time the Carolina parakeet was considered to be extinct. The last wild sighting of the species took place in 1904 in Florida, although reports of Carolina parakeets being seen in the wild persisted until the late 1930s.

Incidentally, the Cincinnati Zoo pays tribute to Lady Jane, Incas, Martha, and other extinct species with its Passenger Pigeon Memorial, which was established in the birds' aviary in 1974.

Hunters also took their toll on wild populations of the thick-billed parrot, which disappeared from the pine forests of Arizona in the early 1900s. It is still found in the western Sierra Madre mountains of Mexico, where it is considered endangered.

Biologists tried to reintroduce the thick-billed parrot to the Chiricahua Mountains of southeastern Arizona from 1986 to 1993 with a flock of 29 adult parrots that had been seized from smugglers by the U.S. Fish and Wildlife Service. As the project progressed, an additional 36 birds were released.

The project was discontinued after a final group of 23 captive-raised birds was released because researchers discovered that most of the captive-raised birds fell victim to hawks shortly after they were released because they lacked the flocking ability required to survive in the

A
Cautionary Tale
Overhunting and irresponsible management led to the demise and extinction of the Carolina parakeet in the early 1900s.

Devotion runs strong between parrots and owners.

wild. Drought and an incurable wasting disease also took their toll on the released birds. Researchers plan to study a wild group of the parrots in Mexico before deciding whether or not to try reintroducing thick-billed parrots to Arizona in the future.

In Puerto Rico, a reintroduction program was begun in 2000 to improve the status of the Puerto Rican Amazon in the wild. Before the reintroduction program began, only ten Puerto Rican Amazons were known to live in the Caribbean National Forest in eastern Puerto Rico. Scientists plan to release chicks bred in aviaries on the island to supplement the wild population. The chicks are released in June and August in order to become acclimated to life in the wild before hurricane season begins in September.

Experts estimate that the Puerto Rican Amazon population may have been as many as 100,000 birds when Christopher Columbus arrived on the island in 1492. By the 1950s, the population had dropped to about 200 birds, and by 1975, it was down to just 13 parrots. In August 1989, the wild population was recorded at 47 birds, but Hurricane Hugo hit the island the following month and destroyed nesting sites in the national forest. Deforestation and competition with other bird species for prime nesting sites are cited as two of the main reasons for the declining number of wild Puerto Rican Amazons.

Pet birds may suffer from boredom and self-mutilation.

The History of Bird-keeping

The practice of keeping birds has a long, rich history, tracing back to China, ancient Egypt, Persia, and early Indian civilizations. The Chinese kept pheasants, the Egyptians had royal zoos that included pigeons, and Persian and Indian writers described parrots and other pet birds in their writings as early as 3,000 years ago.

Bird-keeping was also popular in Greece and Rome. The Greeks were among the first to keep parrots outside of Asia and Africa, and wealthy Romans used mockingbirds in the entryways of their homes to announce visitors. Ravens were especially prized by the Romans for their talking ability. One raven was able to recite the name of Emperor Tiberius and his sons. The bird was killed by a jealous neighbor of its owners, and the man responsible for the killing was lynched by friends of the owner. Many people reportedly paid their respects at the bird's funeral.

The Romans also constructed elaborate garden aviaries, and they were responsible for bringing different types of birds to Great Britain and the European continent. Roman bird-keepers also taught bullfinches to sing elaborate tunes in much the same way roller canaries are taught to sing today.

In medieval Europe, bird-keeping was a pursuit for the wealthy. Kings and queens kept parrots, as did members of the clergy. One parrot that could recite the Lord's Prayer was purchased by a cardinal in Venice for 100 gold pieces, and Pope Martin V, who served as pope from 1417 to 1431, appointed a Keeper of Parrots during his reign in the Vatican.

Among the royal bird owners were King Henry VIII and Marie Antoinette, who both owned African grey parrots, and an African grey that was owned by one of Charles II's mistresses for 40 years is on display in Westminster Abbey in London as an early example of taxidermy.

A wild Senegal parrot faces a world of challenges.

Explorers often sought favor with their royal patrons by providing them with parrots for their royal menageries. Marco Polo reported seeing all types of parrots during his voyages in the 13th century. Italian sailors reported seeing Senegal parrots by the middle of the 15th century, and Christopher Columbus brought Cuban Amazons back to Spain after he discovered the New World in 1492. Part of the New World was referred to as Terra de Papagaios (Land of the Parrots) on maps well into the 16th century, and cartographers often embellished maps of the region with drawings of scarlet macaws.

Spanish conquistadors saw parrots of all sizes as they explored South America. They also discovered a wide range of viewpoints on the importance of parrots in society. Some tribes treated the birds as holy creatures or hosts for reincarnated spirits, while others viewed them merely as a food source.

Portuguese sailors introduced canaries to Europe and made the keeping of pet birds a little more accessible to the general population. Bird-keeping continued to be a largely upper-class hobby until the 1600s, when the Dutch began exporting show canaries to Great Britain.

Halfway around the world, mapmakers documenting the South Pacific region noted Psitacorum Regio, or Region of Parrots, in the South Indian Ocean. Portuguese and Dutch traders made note of some of the parrot species found in the region in the 1500s and 1600s. Don Diego de Prado y Tovar was the first person to describe an Australian bird when he wrote about sulphur-crested cockatoos in his journal of a trip made to New Guinea in 1606. Captain James Cook's explorations of Australia and the South Pacific also documented the existence of parrots in the area.

The roots of today's bird-keeping fancy can trace its beginnings to Victorian Great Britain, when British goldfinches and larks were taken by ship captains to the West Indies, where they were traded for common island species, which were brought back to Great Britain. Troupes of canaries were brought to taverns and coffeehouses to entertain the patrons.

In the United States, pet birds have been kept since colonial days. Martha Washington had a pet parrot, and Dolley Madison and her green parrot had to evacuate Washington, D.C., when the British burned the capital during the War of 1812. Andrew Jackson's parrot, Poll, began to curse so loudly during his funeral service that she had to be removed from the room. Ulysses S. Grant, William McKinley, Theodore Roosevelt, and Calvin Coolidge were among other US presidents who kept parrots in the White House.

Other famous parrot owners include actresses Greta Garbo, Elizabeth Taylor, Bo Derek, and Shelley Duvall, and actors Vincent Price and Robin Williams.

Famous Bird Owners

Calvin Coolidge

Bo Derek

Greta Garbo

Ulysses S. Grant

Andrew Jackson

Vincent Price

Theodore Roosevelt

Elizabeth Taylor

Martha Washington

Robin Williams

Until the early 1980s, most parrots that were kept as pets in the United States were wild-caught animals that were captured in their jungle homelands and imported into this country. Many of these birds were unsatisfactory pets that screamed, bit their owners, or pulled out their feathers. These wild-caught birds also often had long-standing health problems that were difficult to cure.

In the early 1980s, some forward-thinking bird breeders began to realize that wild-caught parrots were not a limitless commodity and that something would have to be done domestically to provide birds for the pet trade. These breeders began to set up breeding pairs of birds, which produced chicks that the breeders hand-raised and sold to pet stores. These hand-raised, domestically bred parrots soon proved to be superior pets to their wild-caught cousins because they were healthier and were accustomed to being around people. Today, domestic-bred parrots make up the bulk of the pet trade because parrots have not been imported into the United States since 1992, when President George H. W. Bush signed the Wild Bird Conservation Act of 1992.

Now that you know a little more about where you can find your new feathered friend and the history of bird-keeping, let's move on to the next chapter in which you'll find more information about picking the parrot that's right for you.

The Birds

It's now time to get down to the business of picking the bird that's right for you. To start off, we'll consider the personalities of many species that are commonly kept as pets.

The first thing you'll want to do when selecting your bird is to try to find one whose personality suits your own. After reviewing the pet bird personality profiles, you'll have a better idea of which species suit your lifestyle and bird-owning tastes.

Visit bird stores in your area to find out if they stock the species you have in mind and take time to get acquainted with the species over several visits. If you have your heart set on an African grey, for example, and the store doesn't offer these birds for sale, ask if

Conure or cockatoo?
The choice is yours.

Indicators of a Healthy Bird

* bird has bright eyes and no nasal discharge
* bird sits upright
* bird doesn't appear thin or weak
* bird is active and moves easily
* bird's legs and vent are clean
* bird's feathers are smooth and free of bald patches
* bird is interested in food and seems to eat well

The bond between pet and owner can happen quickly.

they will have greys in stock in the future. If so, ask if you can be put on a waiting list to be called when the birds come in. If the store won't have greys available in the near future, ask the staff if other stores in your area sell greys or if the staff can recommend a different species to you based on what you found appealing about the African grey personality. In some cases, *Poicephalus* parrots such as Senegals may prove to be a satisfactory alternate choice, while in others, a pionus parrot may fill the bill quite nicely.

When you've selected your species and found birds for sale, look them over carefully. Are some of the birds bolder than the others? Consider those first, because you want a curious, active, robust pet, rather than a shy animal that hides in a corner. Are some birds sitting off by themselves, looking fluffed and cold, or sleeping while their cagemates play? These birds may be ill, so don't consider them when making your pet selection.

If you're lucky, your bird will choose you. It will come over to start playing with you, or it will nudge its head under your hand for a head scratch. If a bird comes over to you, consider it carefully. Birds seem to sense when they've found a kindred spirit, so don't ignore any bird that finds you first!

The following are descriptions of the most commonly kept birds. I've tried to include both the pros and the cons about each species to give you an honest feel for what you're getting into. I'm not trying to discourage anyone from keeping a particular species, but I do want you to know what lies ahead. Bird ownership should be a lifetime commitment, and informed owners are more likely to keep their pet birds for the bird's lifetime than uninformed owners.

Included in each description are comments about the bird's personality, as well as its dietary and housing needs. I've also provided some information on the bird's native habitat, any color variations that occur, and its approximate size. I've also touched on a species' ability to talk and learn tricks and whether or not the species is suited for an apartment or a single-family home.

I broke the price range of the different types of pet birds into three general categories: affordable, moderate, and high. I tried to keep the price ranges as generic as possible to account for regional price differences and changing market conditions. I also wanted to keep the information as current as I could without pinning myself down to actual dollar amounts.

Finally, I've also offered an opinion as to whether or not the species should be kept by novice owners. In most cases, first-time bird owners should start with a smaller species to become accustomed to bird care, then move up to larger species as they gain experience.

You'll notice that I've given weight information for the different species in grams, rather than ounces. Grams are the measurement your avian veterinarian is most likely to use, so it's a good idea to become accustomed to using this weight measure. A gram scale is more precise than one that weighs in ounces for the light weights of most pet birds. Purchase a gram scale for your pet and weigh it regularly to ensure its good health. Weight loss is a prime indicator of illness in pet birds, so keep an eye on your pet's weight.

African Greys

African greys are predominantly gray birds with red tails that measure about 13 inches in length. These highly intelligent birds are widely recognized for their talking abilities, although no bird is guaranteed to talk. Not only are African greys able to amass sizable vocabularies, they are also capable of speaking in different voices, and some birds seem to use words in appropriate contexts. Even my pet grey, who was not noted for her speaking ability while she lived with me, amazed me one night by screaming "Good-Bye!" at the television as a character exited a scene in a video we were watching.

One well-known African grey is Alex, who has been studied by avian behavior expert Dr. Irene Pepperberg for more than 25 years. Pepperberg purchased Alex at a pet store in Chicago as part of a project to study animal intelligence and communication skills. Alex now knows the names of about 100 objects in the laboratory, and he can count to six and name seven different colors and materials. In many cases, Alex uses language in much the same way we do. He can tell Pepperberg or other researchers what is similar or different about two objects that are shown to him, and he uses words to request food, scratches, and other special treatment.

Two species of African greys are commonly available: the Congo grey, which is a larger, lighter gray bird with a black beak and a bright red tail, and the timneh grey, which is a smaller, reddish-gray bird with a reddish-black beak and a maroon tail.

Pet bird owners should be aware that greys are highly tuned in to their owners' moods. These birds know when the people around them are tense or sad, and they react with concerned little looks and noises. Happy owners will often find their greys joining in the celebration with a variety of vocalizations. Allergy sufferers need to know that African greys, like cockatiels and cockatoos, produce powder down, which can cause allergic reactions in some people.

Greys need large cages (24 by 24 by 36 inches is the minimum recommended size), plenty of toys, and ample time out of their cages with their owners. Their diet should consist of pellets, supplemented with a variety of fresh foods. Favorite grey foods include cheese, almonds, corn on the cob, grapes, pomegranates, and bananas. African greys can live up to 50 years with good care.

Congo African grey.

At a Glance

Common name: African grey parrot

Scientific name: *Psittacus erithacus erithacus* (Congo), *P. e. timneh* (timneh)

Other names: Silver parrot, Cameroon parrot, Jacko parrot

Native habitat: African grey parrots live in lowland forests across a wide area of Africa. They can also be found in savannah woodlands and open country during feeding times.

Common color: Depends on subspecies. Congo greys lean toward silver or light gray in color, while timnehs tend toward a dark charcoal gray. Congos have bright red tail feathers and black beaks, while timnehs have maroonish tail feathers and a reddish cast to their beaks.

Other colors: Sometimes a bird with an unusual amount of red feathers will be offered for sale. These birds were once called "King Jackos." Experts are unsure if this coloration is a normal mutation or if it is caused by disease or dietary imbalance.

Length: 9 to 13 inches, depending on subspecies

Weight: 275 to 600 grams, depending on subspecies

Life span: Up to 50 years

Good as single pet? Yes

Good talker? African greys are well-known in the bird world for their ability to imitate voices and noises heard around the home

Good at learning tricks? No

Good cuddler? Sometimes

Apartment dweller or house pet? Both

Relative cost: High

Good for first-time owners? No

Less common than the Congo, the timneh African grey.

Take note: Some African greys can become determined feather-pickers, which can be an extremely difficult habit to break. To reduce the chances of your bird becoming a feather picker, provide it with a healthful diet, plenty of interesting toys, and a stable, calm environment.

Amazons

Amazons are stocky green parrots from Latin America that measure between 10 and 14 inches in length, depending upon the subspecies. They are well known for their independent personalities, their talking and singing skills, and their ability to learn tricks. These birds aren't shy and seem to enjoy showing off. They will get their owners' attention by singing opera, dangling by one foot from their cagetops, whistling "Charge!" or doing whatever it takes to be the center of attention. Popular pet choices include the blue-fronted, the yellow-naped, the double yellow-headed, the red-lored, the orange-winged, and the lilac-crowned Amazons.

Amazons are playful birds that enjoy human companionship, and they will tolerate cuddling on their terms. Be aware, however, that some birds can become strong-willed and somewhat unpredictable, especially during breeding season. Biting is a common behavior at this time. Some people find the Amazon's vocal talents and noise-making ability more than they can handle, so be sure you know what you're getting into in terms of decibels before you adopt an Amazon.

Most Amazons aren't particularly fussy eaters, which has its good and bad points. Amazon owners need to watch the amount of fat their birds consume; Amazons can easily become overweight because they enjoy between-meal snacks. A pelleted diet supplemented with a variety of fresh fruits, vegetables, and other healthy people food, along with a program of regular exercise, should help keep an Amazon in shape.

Lilac-crowned Amazon.

These parrots need roomy cages (at least 24 by 24 by 36 inches) with interesting toys and time out of their cages on playgyms or with their owners to be mentally and physically fit. With good care, Amazons can live 80 years or more.

At a Glance

Common name: Amazon

Scientific name: *Amazona albifrons* (white-fronted Amazon), *A. viridigenalis* (green-cheeked Amazon), *A. finschi* (lilac-crowned Amazon), *A. autumnalis* (red-lored Amazon), *A. festiva* (festive Amazon), *A. aestiva* (blue-fronted Amazon), and *A. ochrocephala* (yellow-crowned Amazon).

Other names: n/a

Native habitat: Amazons are found in forests and in lowland

mountain areas of Mexico and Central and South America.

Common color: Green

Other colors: Lutino and blue mutations are found in some species

Length: 10 to 15 inches

Weight: 240 to 500 grams, depending on species

Life span: Up to 80 years

Good as single pet? Yes

Good talker? Yes

Good at learning tricks? Yes

Good cuddler? Sometimes

A number of Amazon species are readily available as pets.

Apartment dweller or house pet? Most Amazons are better suited for houses than apartments because some can be quite noisy.

Relative cost: High

Good for first-time owners? No

Take note: President William McKinley owned a double yellow-headed Amazon parrot named Washington Post when he was in the White House. The bird was fond of saying "Look at all the pretty girls" whenever women walked past his cage, and he also was quite adept at finishing tunes the president would start whistling for him.

Brotogeris

The *Brotogeris* (bro-toe-JER-us) genus, which includes grey-cheeked, bee bee, and canary-winged parakeets, are 9-inch-tall green birds from Mexico and South America. They are widely recognized in the parrot world for their tame, affectionate natures and their clownish antics. This genus has also been described as "pocket parrots" because of their small sizes and their fondness for hiding in the pockets of their owners' shirts. If it can't find a shirt pocket to hide in, it will burrow under its owner's clothing, so be prepared for this habit if you adopt one of these personable little parrots! One that used to visit my veterinarian's office seemed to enjoy snuggling in the "point" of his owner's V-neck sweaters. He would settle in, close his eyes, and look very contented when he and his owner were in the waiting room.

Brotogeris are also noted for their chewing abilities, so be sure to wear old clothes when allowing your pet to hide in your pockets, and offer it plenty of chewable toys in its cage to satisfy its needs to chew.

Canary-winged parakeet.

Brotogeris make outstanding pets. They can become very attached to their owners and they can learn to talk. *Brotogeris* like to climb, and they are strong fliers, so be sure to keep a pet's wings clipped. Also be aware that some birds may be stubborn when it comes to wanting their way. *Brotogeris* also have a reputation for being loud at times.

Brotogeris like to take baths, and they may bathe in their water bowls if no other water supply is made available. Their diet should include pellets, supplemented with fresh foods such as peas, corn, carrots, cooked beans, bananas, and oranges. They need medium-sized cages (24 by 18 by 36 inches is the recommended cage size) and ample time out of their cages to interact and play with their owners. *Brotogeris* can live about 15 years with good care.

At a Glance

Common name: *Brotogeris*

Scientific name: *Brotogeris versicolorus versicolorus* (white-winged parakeet), *B. v. chiriri* (canary-winged parakeet), *B. pyrrhopterus* (grey-cheeked parakeet), *B. jugularis* (bee bee, Tovi, or orange-chinned parakeet), *B. cyanoptera* (cobalt-winged parakeet), *B.*

chrysopterus (golden-winged parakeet), and *B. sanctithomae* (Tui parakeet).

Other names: n/a

Native habitat: *Brotogeris* species live in arid scrublands and wooded areas throughout Mexico and Central and South America. Many birds can be seen in city parks and botanic gardens in Brazil.

Common color: Green

Other colors: n/a

Length: 9 inches

Weight: 55 to 70 grams

Life span: Up to 15 years

Good as single pet? Yes

Good talker? Sometimes

Good at learning tricks? Sometimes

Good cuddler? Yes

Apartment dweller or house pet? Both

Relative cost: Moderate

Good for first-time owners? Yes

Many of the "pocket parrot" species make excellent pets.

Take note: The grey-cheeked parakeet has also been called the pocket parrot, the orange-flanked parakeet, and the orange-winged parakeet. During importation, it was the most common pet *Brotogeris*.

Caiques

Caiques (ky-EEKs) are South American parrots that measure about 9 inches in length. These intelligent little parrots have good appetites and a tendency to try to eat almost anything that comes near them. They are not shy around strangers and will readily go to any family member. They can be quite vocal, too, and their voices can be moderately loud at times. Look for the white-bellied and the black-headed varieties.

Caiques are noted chewers, so they need to have plenty of toys to destroy. A playgym is also recommended for these active little parrots. You can also channel some of your caique's seemingly endless energy into teaching it tricks. One caique I know enjoys imitating a wind-up toy. His owner gently cuddles him in her hands while she imitates the sound of a key being turned. Then she lets him go, and he hops and bops around until he's "wound down." He goes back to her to repeat the trick, and she tires of it long before he does! Caique owners should be prepared to offer behavioral guidance, too, because some caiques can be stubborn and may get out of control quickly.

White-bellied and black-headed caiques.

Caiques need spacious cages (24 by 24 by 30 inches is the recommended minimum cage size) with a grille to ensure that they don't roll in their cage debris during play. A healthy, happy caique also needs regular interactions with its owner outside of the cage. Their diets should include fresh foods, such as cooked beans and rice, broccoli, and sprouted peas and beans, along with pellets. Because of their high energy levels, caiques have healthy appetites, so be sure to keep their food bowls filled! Be aware that caiques are prone to playing in their food bowls, and they're known to take frequent baths in their water bowls, too. Caiques can live 25 years with good care.

At a Glance

Common name: Caique

Scientific name: *Pionites* species

Other names: n/a

Native habitat: South America

Common color: Green

Other colors: n/a

Length: 9 inches

Weight: 170 to 190 grams

Life span: Up to 15 years

Good as single pet? Yes

Good talker? Sometimes

Good at learning tricks? Yes

Good cuddler? Sometimes

Apartment dweller or house pet? Both

Relative cost: Moderate

Good for first-time owners? Yes

The Showoffs

These species are likely to learn tricks:

Amazons

Caiques

Cockatoos

Lovebirds

Macaws

Quakers

Take note: One of the caique's most endearing behaviors is the hopscotch-like skipping gait it frequently uses. Allow your caique plenty of out-of-cage time to give it ample opportunity to hop around your home.

Canaries

Canaries are small cage birds that have been kept in captivity since the 1400s and are thoroughly domesticated. Commonly kept varieties include the American singer, the Border fancy, and the red factor.

Breeders concentrate on different attributes in their canary lines. Some breed canaries for shape and stance, while others want color canaries that are developed for their colorful feathers (along with the familiar yellow, canaries can also come in white, red, orange, or brownish colors). Still others breed song canaries for their lovely singing abilities.

Canaries are not noted for being interactive pets. They are content to remain in their cages most of the time. Because they spend so much time in their cages, a good-sized cage is recommended. Rectangular cages with perches placed on either end are preferred to provide a canary with optimal exercise opportunities.

If you want a singing canary, you will have to locate a male. Make arrangements with the breeder or store to return the bird if it proves to be a non-singer. Keep in mind that males sing to attract females. If canaries are kept in pairs, males won't sing. Males won't sing during the summer because that is the molting period. If your bird stops singing at any other time, contact your avian veterinarian for an evaluation because this can indicate illness.

At a Glance

Common name: Canary

Scientific name: *Serinus canarius domesticus*

Native habitat: Canary Islands, but all pet birds available today are domestically bred.

Common color: Yellow

Other colors: Red-orange, pink, white, variegated shades of brown

Length: 4 to 8 inches

Weight: 12 to 29 grams

Lifespan: Up to 20 years

Good as single pet? Yes

Good talker? No

Good at learning tricks? No

Good cuddler? No

Apartment dweller or house pet? Both

Relative cost: Low

Good for first-time owners? Yes

Take note: Most canaries do not like to be handled. They also do not require regular interaction with their owners as many parrot species do.

Singing abilities set canaries aside from most other pet birds.

Cockatiels

Cockatiels are the second-most popularly kept pet bird in the world. These slender, crested parrots from Australia are known for their whistling ability and their mellow temperaments. Their small size (between 11 and 14 inches in length), personable nature, and easy care requirements make them good choices for a first bird.

In the wild, cockatiels are gray birds with yellow heads and orange cheek patches. From this wild coloration, cockatiel breeders have developed a number of color mutations, including lutino, pied, albino, and cinnamon. Multiple mutation birds are now available that combine two or more of these mutations.

Potential bird owners with allergies need to know that cockatiels produce powder down, a dusty white substance that creates allergic symptoms in some people. Some cockatiels are prone to biting, too. If your bird develops this habit, consult your avian veterinarian or an avian behaviorist for suggestions on how it can be stopped.

Cockatiels need a varied diet that includes pellets, fresh fruits, and vegetables. Some foods that are popular with cockatiels include corn, broccoli, spinach, cooked rice and beans, and well-cooked hard-boiled egg, all offered in cockatiel-size portions.

A perennial favorite, the cockatiel.

As with parakeets, cockatiels can easily become seed-only eaters, so make sure your bird is introduced to a variety of healthy foods when it is young. Provide plenty of fresh water, too, to ensure your pet's good health.

Cockatiels are notorious for their whistling ability. Many birds seem to quickly learn tunes, such as *The Andy Griffith Show* theme. Some birds also learn to talk, but many seem to prefer whistling to talking.

Cockatiels can become quite bonded to their owners. Several I know follow their owners around the house with dog-like devotion. Other family members are aware of this habit and make sure not to step on these loyal little birds.

A cockatiel's cage should be roomy enough to accommodate both its crest and its long tail. The cage should measure about 18 by 18 by 24 inches, with $1/2$- to $3/4$-inch bar spacing. The cage should be large enough for the bird to climb, play, and flap its wings, and you should also allow your cockatiel time out of its cage for further exercise on a playgym or cagetop playpen. Cockatiels can live more than 20 years with good care.

At a Glance

Common name: Cockatiel

Scientific name: *Nymphicus hollandicus*

Other names: Quarrion, cockatoo-parrot

Native habitat: Cockatiels can be found in the arid interior of Australia

Common color: Gray

Other colors: Lutino, pied, cinnamon, pearl, whiteface, fallow, albino, and yellowface

Length: 12 inches

Weight: 80 to 100 grams

Life span: Up to 32 years

Good as single pet? Yes

Good talker? Although many cockatiels are noted for their whistling ability rather than their talking prowess, some do learn to talk well.

Good at learning tricks? Sometimes

Good cuddler? Yes

Apartment dweller or house pet? Both

Relative cost: Affordable to moderate

Good for first-time owners? Yes

Cockatiels come in the normal coloration as well as mutations.

Take note: Gender-based traits are frequently seen in cockatiels. Many experts believe that male cockatiels are better able to learn to whistle and talk, while female cockatiels seem to be more cuddly and playful.

Cockatoos

Cockatoos come from Australia. These crested white or pink birds combine a distinctive look with a frequently cuddly personality. They measure between 12 and 28 inches in length, depending upon the species.

Although the cockatoo's cuddliness is initially appealing, it can become frustrating for both bird and owner if the owner doesn't realize what he or she is getting into before the bird comes home. Cockatoos require a great deal of attention from their owners to be content pets, and most people aren't equipped to offer the amount of attention these large parrots require. If the bird feels it's being neglected by its owner, it may scream, pull its feathers, or even mutilate its chest or wing tips. All these behaviors can be extremely difficult to change once the bird has begun them.

Another drawback with some species is their tendency to be possessive of their owners, especially during breeding season. They can bite the person in the home they perceive as their "mate," and these bites can cause severe injuries. One bird I know is capable of giving his owner a black eye during breeding season. He has bitten her badly enough that her doctor feared she was a domestic violence victim. Her husband wasn't the abuser, but her bird was.

Potential pet owners also need to know that cockatoos produce powder down, which can cause allergic reactions in some people. This powdery substance helps the birds keep their feathers in condition, but it can also be irritating to a sensitive person's eyes, nose, and throat.

Cockatoos need large, secure cages because they are clever enough to become talented escape artists. Some birds can even learn how to disassemble their entire cages! A recommended cage for a cockatoo measures 36 by 36 by 48 inches. Additional keyed padlocks are often required on the cage door to ensure that the cockatoo stays in its cage because they can learn to open combination locks or other fasteners.

A cockatoo's diet should include pellets supplemented with fresh fruits and vegetables, such as green peppers, bananas, grapes, tomatillos, peas, brussel sprouts, and corn on the cob. With good care, cockatoos can live 40 years or more.

Feathered Caretakers

Cockatiels have been recognized for their ability to sense certain medical conditions in their owners, such as the onset of migraine headaches or epileptic seizures. In the case of seizures, the birds have been seen quietly rocking on their perches just before the seizure began. With migraines, they are prone to cuddle up with the person suffering the migraine. When the owner is well, however, the cockatiel prefers to spend time with another person in the home. They exhibit this behavior only when their owner becomes ill.

At a Glance

Common name: Cockatoo

Scientific name: *Cacatua leadbeateri* (Leadbeater's or Major Mitchell's cockatoo), *C. sulphurea* (lesser sulphur-crested cockatoo), *C. galerita* (sulphur-crested cockatoo), *C. moluccensis* (Moluccan or salmon-crested cockatoo), *C. goffini* (Goffin's cockatoo), *C. alba* (umbrella Cockatoo), and *Eolophus rosecapillus* (rose-breasted cockatoo or galah).

Other names: Several species go by more than one name. These include the Leadbeater's or Major Mitchell's, the Moluccan or salmon crested, and the rose breasted or galah.

Native habitat: Cockatoo species can be found in a wide variety of habitats, such as savannah woodlands, open grasslands, arid woodlands, and lowland forests of Australia, Indonesia, Tasmania, and New Guinea.

Common color: White or pink

Other colors: Black cockatoos are seen in zoos and in the wild. These species are not commonly available in the pet trade.

Length: 10 to 20 inches

Weight: 220 to 1200 grams, depending on species

Life span: Up to 40 years

Good as single pet? Yes, but requires a great deal of patience and attention from owner

Good talker? No

Good at learning tricks? sometimes

Good cuddler? Cockatoos are well known in the bird world for being "feathered teddy bears."

Apartment dweller or house pet? Thanks to their ability to scream, most cockatoos are recommended for house pet situations or aviary living.

Relative cost: High

Good for first-time owners? No

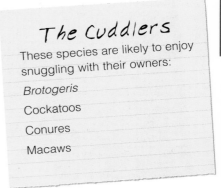

The Cuddlers

These species are likely to enjoy snuggling with their owners:

Brotogeris

Cockatoos

Conures

Macaws

An umbrella cockatoo displays its impressive crest.

The rose-breasted is one of the more colorful cockatoos.

Take note: Age and gender can be determined to a degree in many cockatoo species. Female birds have tan-to-reddish irises, while males have dark brown or black irises. Young birds less than a year old have brown eyes.

Conures

Conures are small to medium-sized South American parrots that range in length from 8 to 18 inches. These active, curious birds come in a wide range of colors, from brown to green and red to orange to yellow. Some conures can be fair talkers, while others like to cuddle with their owners, and still others enjoy showing off and being the center of attention.

A small bird park near our home has a variety of birds from conures to macaws on display. People can walk around the park (an enclosed aviary) and feed or play with the parrots. Staff members supervise the birds and the visitors to minimize injury to both. The conures are among the most popular. Visitors seem drawn to them because they are brightly colored and animated. Their size also isn't as intimidating as the macaws or cockatoos that are on display in other parts of the park.

These parrots have a few traits that first-time owners need to be aware of. Conures are well known for their chewing abilities, and they will chew on whatever they can get their beaks on, whether it's a parrot chew toy or your antique bookcase. Many conures are quite noisy, so choose your pet carefully if noise considerations are an issue. Conures love to take baths, which means they will need access to clean, fresh water, either in a special birdie bathtub in their cages or by standing under the faucet in the shower or sink (be sure to monitor the water temperature carefully so your pet isn't scalded if you allow it to bathe under the faucet). Finally, some conure species fall asleep on their backs, often on the cage floor or in their food bowls. Although this is completely normal behavior, it can be downright startling for a new bird owner who hasn't seen the behavior before. Many new conure owners mistakenly believe their pets are seriously ill or dead when they first see the birds asleep on the floor of the cage, but it's typical behavior for many conure species.

If you choose a conure, make sure to give it a spacious cage because it will need lots of room. A recommended minimum cage size for a small conure would be 24 inches all around, with $^1/_2$- to $^3/_4$-inch bar spacing. Larger species would, of course, need a larger cage.

Your conure will need time out of its cage as well, and this time can be spent on a playgym under your supervision. Conures are very fun-loving birds, and many quickly learn tricks. Pellets, supplemented with healthy people food, such as fresh fruits and vegetables, and plenty of fresh water, make a healthful conure diet. Conures can live more than 20 years with proper care.

At a Glance

Common name: Conure

Scientific name: *Aratinga acuticaudata* (blue-crowned conure), *A. finschi* (Finsch's conure), *A. wagleri* (red-fronted or Wagler's conure), *A. mitrata* (mitred conure), *A. jendaya* (jenday conure), *A. solstitialis* (sun conure), *A. weddellii* (dusky conure), *A. canicularis* (halfmoon or Petz's conure), *A. aurea* (peach-fronted or golden-crowned conure), *A. erythrogenys* (cherry-headed or red-masked conure), *Pyrrhura frontalis* (maroon-bellied conure), *P. molinae* (green-cheeked conure), *Nandayus nenday* (nanday conure), *Cyanoliseus patagonus* (Patagonian conure), and *Enicognathus leptorhynchus* (slender-billed conure).

The vividly feathered blue-crowned conure.

Other names: Some conure species are known by more than one name. Examples of these include the halfmoon or Petz's, the peach front or golden crown, and the cherry head or red mask.

Native habitat: Conures can be found in a wide variety of habitats in Central and South America, including tropical rainforest, inland caatinga (a specialized arid vegetation community characterized by thorny scrub, cacti, and other succulents), and cliff faces.

Common color: Varies, depending on species. Color

Part 1

Conures are noted for their playful antics.

combinations include green and red; blue and green; gold, orange, and green; and gold and green.

Other colors: n/a

Length: 9 to 18 inches

Weight: 80 to 130 grams

Life span: Up to 25 years

Good as single pet? Yes

Good talker? No

Good at learning tricks? Yes

Good cuddler? Some species are, others aren't

Apartment dweller or house pet? Some species are suitable for apartment living, while others are recommended for houses or aviary situations.

Relative cost: Affordable to moderate

Good for first-time owners? Yes

Take note: Some experts believe that conures are the most successful group of parrots to evolve on the planet. More than 100 species and subspecies of conure have been identified.

The Loudmouths

These species may have voices that are too loud for apartment living or other close quarters:

Amazons

Cockatoos

Conures

Macaws

Eclectus

Eclectus are solid 14-inch-tall parrots from the South Pacific. The males and females are sexually dimorphic, which means that males and females look different. Male birds are green with orange beaks, while females have purple and red feathers with black beaks.

Eclectus are not usually cuddly parrots, but they will enjoy sitting on a perch near their owners or perching on their owners' hands. Although they are not noted for their talking ability, some birds will learn a few words or phrases. One female I know sings along with country music when her owners play the radio, while another enthusiastically says "Yummy!" when her owner feeds her in the morning.

Female eclectus may become moody during breeding season after they become sexually mature at about four years of age, or they may demonstrate an increased interest in trying to go to nest. Females are traditionally more aggressive than males.

Eclectus have different vitamin A requirements than other parrot species. Ask your avian veterinarian for suggestions on the best diet for your eclectus. To keep yours healthy and content, give it a large cage (24 by 24 by 36 inches is the minimum recommended size), a variety of toys and time out of its cage, either on a playgym or on a perch near you. With good care, eclectus can live about 20 years.

At a Glance

Common name: Eclectus

Scientific name: *Eclectus roratus roratus* (grand eclectus), *E. r. polychloros* (red-sided eclectus), *E. r. vosmaeri* (Vosmaeri eclectus), and *E. r. solomonensis* (Solomon Island eclectus)

Other names: n/a

Native habitat: Eclectus species live in lowland forests and clumps of trees found in savannahs throughout New Guinea, Australia, and some South Pacific islands.

Common color: Females are red and blue-violet with black beaks, while males are green and red with reddish-orange beaks

Male and female eclectus parrots.

Other colors: n/a

Length: 14 inches

The zebra finch is the most commonly kept finch.

The Quieter Ones

These species are suitable for apartment living because they are relatively quiet:

African greys

Cockatiels

Eclectus

Lovebirds

Parakeets

Pionus

Weight: 380 to 525 grams

Life span: Up to 20 years

Good as single pet? Yes

Good talker? No

Good at learning tricks? No

Good cuddler? No

Apartment dweller or house pet? Both

Relative cost: High

Good for first-time owners? No

Take note: Early explorers who discovered the eclectus initially believed they had found two different species of birds because the males and females look so different.

Finches

Finches are small, active cage birds that come from Asia, Africa, and Australia. They are well suited to community aviaries or flights, although a pair can easily be kept in a cage. Keeping a single pet finch is not recommended because these small birds enjoy each other's company and because finches rarely interact well with people.

Some species are noted for their colorful feathers, while others sing pleasant songs. Although some birds have been known to enjoy sitting on their owners' shoulders, most finches are admired from afar.

Because finches spend most of their time inside their cages, a large rectangular cage is recommended. Place perches on opposite ends of the cage to provide maximum flying distance for your finches.

At a Glance

Common name: Depends on species

Scientific name: *Chloebia* spp., *Poelphila* spp., *Zonaeginthus* spp., *Stizoptera* spp., *Lonchura* spp.

Native habitat: Wild finches can be found in the forests and grasslands of Asia, Africa, and Australia.

Common color: Depends on species. Finches can be as drably colored as the black-and-white owl finch or as bright as a Lady Gouldian, which has been described as "a stained glass window with feathers."

Length: 3 to 8 inches

Weight: 10 to 20 grams

Lifespan: 5 to 17 years

Good as single pet? Perhaps, but better suited for life in a flock or community aviary

Good talker? No

Good at learning tricks? No

Good cuddler? No

Apartment dweller or house pet? Both

Relative cost: Low to moderate

Good for first-time owners? Some species are. Check with your bird store staff for recommendations.

Take note: Some finch species are high strung. These birds may benefit from plenty of hiding places in their cages, such as nest boxes, bird-safe potted plants or a terracotta flowerpot turned on its side on the cage bottom. Make sure to secure the pot to ensure it doesn't accidentally roll over onto your finch.

Lories and Lorikeets

Lories and lorikeets are active, curious parrots from the South Pacific that measure about 12 inches in length. The distinction between lories and lorikeets is made by tail length. Birds with short, square tails are referred to as lories, while those with long, pointed tails are considered lorikeets. Commonly kept species include the rainbow, the chattering, the black cap, the dusky, the blue streak, and the Goldie's.

Lories and lorikeets are available in a variety of sizes and colors to suit almost anyone's taste. Potential owners need to know that these brush-tongued parrots are specialty feeders, requiring a diet of nectar and fruit rather than the common parrot fare of pellets. Because of their specialized dietary requirements, they are not recommended for first-time bird owners.

The rainbow lory, colorful and common.

Some species of lories and lorikeets are likely to talk, and all are ready and willing to play and entertain themselves and their owners. The lory exhibit is one of the more popular stops for visitors to the San Diego Wild Animal Park. Zoo visitors seem to enjoy watching these colorful parrots dart about their enclosures. For a small fee, you can purchase a cup of nectar to feed the lories. After the nectar is gone, it's fun to stay inside the exhibit and watch the birds feed from other nectar cups and play.

These birds enjoy sleeping in nest boxes even when they aren't breeding, so they will need to have an enclosed sleeping space attached to their cages, which should measure at least 24 by 24 by 36 inches. A playgym is also recommended for these acrobatic birds.

Lories and lorikeets like to bathe regularly, and they may bathe in their water bowls if no other bathtub is provided. Their fruit-and-nectar-based diets cause them to produce messy droppings, although powdered diets are available that make keeping these birds easier. Lories and lorikeets can live about 15 years with good care.

At a Glance

Common name: Lory or lorikeet

Scientific name: *Chalcopsitta atra* (black lory), *C. duivenbodei* (Duyvenbode's lory), *Eos bornea* (red or Moluccan lory), *E. squamata* (violet-necked lory), *E. reticulata* (blue-streaked lory), *Lorius garrulus* (chattering lory), *L. lory* (black-capped lory), *Pseudeos fuscata* (dusky lory), *Trichoglossus haematodus* (rainbow lory), and *T. goldiei* (Goldie's lorikeet).

Other names: n/a

Native habitat: Lories and lorikeets live in coastal zones, in montane forests, and in trees on the edge of forests and savannahs in Indonesia, New Guinea, and Australia.

Common color: Lories and lorikeets are available in a wide variety of colors, including red, green, blue, and black. Many species sport multi-colored feathers.

Other colors: n/a

Length: 7 to 12 inches

Weight: 250 grams

Life span: Up to 15 years

Good as single pet? Yes

Good talker? Sometimes

Good at learning tricks? Sometimes

Good cuddler? Sometimes

Apartment dweller or house pet? Both

Relative cost: Moderate to high

Good for first-time owners? No

Take note: Even with the advent of powdered diets for lories and lorikeets, these birds still need daily access to nectar and fresh fruit to maintain their good health.

Lovebirds

Lovebirds are playful, acrobatic, energetic 5-inch-tall parrots that come in a variety of colors, including blue, green, and yellow. In the wild, lovebirds are found across a wide range in central and southern Africa and on the island of Madagascar. Three species—the peach-faced, the Fischer's, and the masked—are most commonly kept as pets.

While you might expect lovebirds to be loving little pets, these active little parrots really can be aggressive toward other birds and people. They require daily handling to retain their sweet pet qualities. A friend's pair—Heckle and Jeckle—far prefer each other's company to spending time with him.

Lovebirds are active but not necessarily lovable.

Keeping a single pet lovebird will increase your chances of having a handleable pet you can enjoy because the bird will bond with you rather than with another lovebird. If you choose to keep a single lovebird, make sure to pay it plenty of attention because the bird will depend upon you to meet its social needs. Although many people think you have to keep lovebirds in pairs for the birds to be happy, the truth is you can successfully keep a single pet lovebird if you're willing to provide for its social needs.

Lovebirds love to chew, and one of their favorite things to rip up is paper. Some species like to shred paper and tuck it into their rump feathers. If you see your lovebird do this, chances are that you have a female bird that's ready to build a nest. Be sure to provide your pet with plenty of chewable toys in its cage to satisfy its chewing needs.

Part 1

Despite their small size, lovebirds need spacious cages in which they can burn off their high energy by climbing and exercising. They can also be taught to perform tricks. The minimum size for a lovebird cage would be 18 by 18 by 24 inches, with $^3/_8$- to $^7/_{16}$-inch bar spacing. Playing with toys will also help them use up some of their energy. Lovebirds also enjoy bathing, so make sure to offer your pet an opportunity to bathe, either in its cage or under a light stream of warm water in the sink. Supervise your pet when it's bathing outside its cage to ensure the water doesn't become too hot.

A good quality lovebird diet should include pellets supplemented with fresh fruits and vegetables, such as strawberries, apricots (with the pits removed), bananas, and dark leafy greens (your lovebird may decide to roll around in the greens before eating, combining three of a lovebird's favorite activities: bathing, eating, and playing). With proper care, a lovebird can live about 12 years.

At a Glance

Common name: Lovebird

Scientific name: *Agapornis roseicollis* (peach-faced lovebird), *A. fischeri* (Fischer's lovebird), *A. personata* (masked lovebird), *A. lilianae* (Nyasa lovebird), *A. cana* (Madagascar lovebird), *A. taranta* (black-winged lovebird), *A. nigrigenis* (black-cheeked lovebird), *A. pullaria* (red-faced lovebird), and *A. swinderniana* (black-collared lovebird).

Other names: n/a

Native habitat: Lovebirds are found in highland and lowland forests, in savannah woodlands and lightly timbered grasslands, and often near cultivated fields across Africa and Madagascar.

Common color: Varies according to species. Colors include green, blue, yellow, and a wide variety of mutations.

Other colors: n/a

Length: 5 to 6 $^1/_2$ inches

The Acrobats

These species have high energy levels, which means they need large cages and lots of toys:

Caiques

Conures

Lories and lorikeets

Lovebirds

Parakeets

Parrotlets

Quakers

Senegals

A blue mutation of the black-masked lovebird.

Weight: 50 to 70 grams

Life span: Up to 12 years

Good as single pet? Although many new bird owners believe lovebirds must be kept in pairs, they can be quite content as single pets.

Good talker? No

Good at learning tricks? Yes

Good cuddler? No

Apartment dweller or house pet? Both

Relative cost: Affordable

Good for first-time owners? Yes

Take note: Don't house peach-faced lovebirds with Fischer's or masked lovebirds because territorial fights could break out between the birds.

Macaws

Macaws are the largest commonly kept cage birds. They hail from South America and are available in a rainbow of colors, including green, blue, and red. Macaws measure between 12 and 36 inches in length, depending on species. Commonly kept species of large macaws include the blue and gold, the military, the scarlet, and the greenwing. Commonly kept miniature macaw species include the Hahn's, the noble, the yellow collar, and the severe.

Macaws can learn to talk or to perform a wide variety of tricks, including waving, playing dead, turning somersaults, and dancing. They are often featured in bird shows because of their ability to learn these tricks, their large size, and their showy plumage. These highly intelligent parrots are great chewers, so you must provide them with a ready supply of appropriate chew toys.

The larger species can intimidate some owners with their strong wills, and they are not recommended for first-time bird owners. Their beaks can also be powerful, as a customer at a pet store in Orange County, California, learned a few years ago. She required plastic surgery to repair damage done to her face and ear after the store's mascot, a scarlet macaw, bit her several times.

Large macaws need to have guidelines established for them as soon as they come home from the pet store or breeder in order to learn how to behave appropriately in the home. Otherwise, they can learn to scream, bite, or otherwise manipulate their owners and the home environment to suit their needs. This results in a poorly behaved bird and a frustrated owner, and the bird-owner relationship suffers.

The scarlet macaw, in all its spectacular glory.

Macaws need large cages to accommodate their large sizes. The minimum size for a macaw cage would be 36 by 36 by 60 inches. Their diet should include pellets, supplemented with fresh fruits and vegetables, such as mangos, kiwi fruit, bananas, cooked yams, peas, and watermelon. With good care, macaws can live 50 years or more.

At a Glance

Common name: Macaw

Scientific name: *Ara ararauna* (blue and gold macaw), *A. militaris* (military macaw), *A. ambigua* (Buffon's macaw), *A. macao* (scarlet macaw), *A. chloroptera* (green-winged macaw), *A. severa* (chestnut-fronted or severe macaw), *A. auricollis* (yellow-collared macaw), *A. manilata* (red-bellied macaw), *A. nobilis* (noble or Hahn's macaw), and *Anodorhynchus hyacinthinus* (hyacinth macaw).

Other names: n/a

Native habitat: Macaw species are found in dry forest and open woodland in Central and South America. They also live in humid lowland forests, palm swamps, and on forest-fringed savannahs.

Common color: green, red and green, red and yellow, blue, and blue and gold

Other colors: n/a

Length: 12 to 36 inches

Weight: 220 to 1530 grams, depending on species

Life span: Up to 50 years

Good as single pet? Yes

Good talker? Sometimes

Good at learning tricks? Yes

Good cuddler? Sometimes

Apartment dweller or house pet? Most macaws are recommended for houses or aviaries because the birds' ability to vocalize, along with the size of their cages and accessories, may not lend themselves to the small spaces of an apartment.

Relative cost: Moderate to high

Good for first-time owners? No

Take note: The hyacinth is the largest and most expensive of the macaws.

Though rare as a pet, the hyacinth macaw is a gentle parrot.

Parakeets

The bird that is commonly called a parakeet in America is typically called a budgerigar or budgie in other parts of the world and by many experienced bird-keepers. The small and very popular pet bird originates from Australia and has been kept in captivity for more than 150 years. Originally available only in its "wild" green-and-yellow coloration, parakeet breeders have now developed more than 50 color mutations, including blue, mauve, lutino (yellow), and gray.

Two varieties of parakeet are available: the English and the American. English parakeets are most commonly seen on the show circuit, and they are larger and more sedate than their American cousins. American parakeets are smaller and more active than English parakeets, but either variety can make a wonderful pet.

Parakeets are noted for their talking ability, but their small voices can sometimes be difficult for owners to hear, so listen carefully if you hear your pet seeming to mutter to itself. It may be practicing its vocabulary. These active, fairly quiet little parrots can be kept singly, in pairs, or in community aviaries. They are good candidates for first birds because of their small sizes (about 7 inches in length), their playful natures, and their easy care routines. Other positive aspects of the parakeet personality include ease of handling, a low potential for biting, and the possibility of having a bird that enjoys cuddling and interacting with its owner. Some parakeets like to have their heads scratched, while others enjoy having their cheek patches petted. My boyfriend's daughter's bird, Andre, will deliberately lean into her finger through the cage bars. If he's out of his cage and needs a scratch, he will walk up to her hand and position himself so her finger is over the spot that needs scratching. Parakeets are not particularly destructive birds, especially if given a variety of chew toys in their cages.

Small, colorful, and charming, the parakeet is always a favorite.

Although they are often recommended for first-time bird owners, more experienced bird-keepers also appreciate the parakeet's endearing pet qualities. The parakeet's size and personality make it an ideal pet for almost anyone, which may be the reason why it's the most popularly kept species of pet bird in the United States and why it has a large following in Great Britain and Australia, too.

Despite their small sizes, parakeets need a good-sized cage in order to exercise properly. A good-sized parakeet cage would measure 18 by 18 by 24 inches, with $^3/_8$- to $^7/_{16}$-inch bar spacing. They should also receive daily time out of their cages during which they can play and interact with their owners. This can be best accomplished by setting up a playgym for the bird in your family room or TV room. By placing your bird on the playgym while you watch television or spend time with your family, your bird feels like it's part of your family flock, which helps meet its social needs. A single pet parakeet must have time out of the cage because it can become lonely if neglected.

If you think you will be unable to meet your parakeet's social needs, consider adopting a pair of birds. Keep in mind that a pair of birds often will bond to each other more closely than they will with their human owners. Also note that you should bring both birds home at the same time and introduce them to their new cage together in order to prevent one bird from becoming a territorial bully toward newcomers. If you purchase a pair of birds instead of a single pet, make sure to purchase a cage that's large enough to hold both birds and all their accessories comfortably.

A balanced parakeet diet includes pellets supplemented with an assortment of fresh fruits and vegetables. Parakeets especially enjoy leafy greens, grated carrots, raw broccoli, and apple slices. Make sure to offer your pet parakeet-size portions of these fresh foods because larger pieces can sometimes seem frightening to these small birds.

Offer your parakeet a variety of fresh foods when it is young because these birds tend to become seed-only eaters if not introduced to a more healthful diet early in their lives. Make sure your parakeet also has access to plenty of fresh water.

First-time bird owners need to know that parakeets are unlikely to eat from hooded or covered food bowls, so be sure to provide your pet with an open dish for its pellets. With good care, a pet parakeet can live 18 to 20 years.

At a Glance

Common name: Budgerigar

Scientific name: *Melopsittacus undulatus*

Other names: budgerigar, budgie, green grass parakeet, warbling grass parakeet, shell parakeet, zebra parrot, and scallop parrot

Native habitat: Parakeets can be found in the arid interior of Australia

Common color: Green

Other colors: A wide variety, including blue, yellow, sky blue, dark green, olive green, white, cobalt, mauve, violet, lutino, albino, cinnamon, pied, fallow, gray, opaline, and yellowface.

Length: 7 inches

Weight: 30 to 60 grams

Life span: Up to 18 years

Good as single pet? Yes

Good talker? Parakeets are among the best mimics in the bird world

Good at learning tricks? Yes

Good cuddler? Yes

Apartment dweller or house pet? Both

Note the blue cere (above the beak) of the male parakeet.

The Talkers

These species are likely to learn to talk well:

African greys

Amazons

Parakeets

Quaker parakeets

Relative cost: Affordable

Good for first-time owners? Yes

Take note: Adult parakeets can sometimes be sexed visually. Male parakeets often have a blue cere (the featherless skin above the bird's beak), while the cere on female parakeets is usually pink or brownish.

Parrotlets

Parrotlets are spunky, playful birds from Latin America. These bold 5-inch-tall parrots need close supervision when they are out of their cages to ensure their safety because these little birds don't seem to realize how small they are and how prone they may be to accidental injury from other members of the household.

Parrotlets are comical little birds that expect to spend time with their owners when people are around. A female Pacific parrotlet I know, Doodle, ruled the roost at the home of some dear friends. She was more demanding than the family's pet cockatoo, and she had to be involved in all family activities. She supervised meal preparation while riding on my friend's shoulder around the kitchen, and she required her own place at the table (a portable perch on wheels that was drawn up close to the table). Her mate, Yankee, was far less demanding. He was content to watch household activities from the safety of his cage rather than actively taking part in it.

Although they enjoy human companionship, parrotlets have little trouble entertaining themselves while their human family is away. They enjoy learning tricks, and some can develop vocabularies of 100 words or more.

Parrotlets should be housed in medium-size cages that contain a variety of toys and several perches at different levels in the cage so these active little birds can play, climb, and exercise. The cage should measure no less than 18 by 18 by 18 inches, and it should have bar spacing between $^3/_8$ and $^7/_{16}$ inches.

Pacific parrotlet, one of several spunky parrotlets available.

Parrotlets enjoy a weekly bath, which can be offered by placing a shallow dish of warm water into the bird's cage or by allowing the bird to bathe under a faucet of gently running warm water. Play lifeguard if your parrotlet bathes outside its cage to be sure the water temperature stays cool enough to prevent burns or scalds.

Parrotlets should eat a diet that contains pellets supplemented with fresh fruits and vegetables. Some of their favorite foods include whole-grain bread, cooked beans, cooked white or sweet potatoes, tomatillos, cranberries, green peppers, and brussel sprouts. Because they are such active birds, they require what may seem like a large amount of food in comparison to their small bodies. Be sure to keep your pet's food bowl well stocked to ensure its energy level remains high and it maintains good health.

Keep in mind that parrotlets may not eat readily from covered food bowls, so be sure to provide your pet with an open food dish. With good care, a parrotlet can live more than ten years.

At a Glance

Common name: Parrotlet

Scientific name: *Forpus passerinus* (green-rumped parrotlet), *F. xanthopterygius* (blue-winged parrotlet), *F. conspicillatus* (spectacled parrotlet), *F. coelestis* (Pacific parrotlet), and *F. xanthops* (yellow-faced parrotlet).

Other names: Blue-winged lovebird

Native habitat: Parrotlets are found in tropical rainforests and arid regions of Mexico, South America, and some Caribbean islands

Common color: Green

Other colors: Blue and lutino

Length: 5 inches

Weight: 20 to 30 grams

Life span: Up to ten years

Good as single pet? Better kept in pairs

Good talker? No

Good at learning tricks? No

Good cuddler? Sometimes

Apartment dweller or house pet? Both

Relative cost: Affordable

Good for first-time owners? Yes

Take note: Parrotlets are sexually dimorphic, which means the males and females can be sexed visually. Male parrotlets have intense blue markings, while females' blue markings are of a lighter shade.

Pionus

Pionus (pie-OH-nus) are stocky, medium-size parrots that measure between 9 and 12 inches in length. These little-known Latin American natives are fairly quiet and possess sweet dispositions. I think they are among the most overlooked parrots. Part of the problem may be their laid-back demeanor. They don't attract attention like a macaw or Amazon does. Some people may be put off by their seemingly drab plumage. But if you take a second look at these birds, you'll see a virtual rainbow of colors in their feathers. You'll also see a wonderful pet bird.

Pionus enjoy bathing and climbing, and they are noted for their chewing abilities. These affectionate birds enjoy spending time with people, but they don't require a great deal of handling or cuddling to remain content. Although they aren't known for their talking abilities, some pionus can develop fair vocabularies.

Pionus may wheeze when excited, and some can be high strung and somewhat nervous.

Fortunately, they can usually be talked out of their wheezing fits with soothing tones and reassuring words. They do not tolerate heat and/or humidity well and may become stressed easily.

Pionus enjoy regular baths, so make sure to mist them often with clean, warm water or take them in the shower with you to fulfill their bathing needs. If you use a spray bottle to mist your bird, make sure to mark it as the bird's shower bottle so it won't be used for household chemicals, which could harm your bird if sprayed on its feathers.

Pionus require large cages and a diet of pellets, supplemented with fresh foods, such as apples, cooked sweet potatoes, pomegranates, broccoli, and peas. Some birds can become overweight easily, so it's best to feed your pionus a low-fat diet. Their cages should measure 24 by 24 by 36 inches with bar spacing between $^3/_4$-inch and 1 inch. They can live up to 20 years with good care.

At a Glance

Common name: Pionus

Scientific name: *Pionus senilis* (white-capped pionus), *P. chalcopterus* (bronze-winged pionus), *P. maximiliani* (Maximilian's or scaly-headed pionus), *P. menstruus* (blue-headed pionus), and *P. fuscus* (dusky pionus).

Other names: n/a

Native habitat: The different species of pionus are found in lightly timbered areas, open woodlands, rainforests, and lowland forests in Mexico, Central, and South America.

Common color: Pionus are rather drab birds. Their predominant color is green or grayish blue, accented with blue.

Other colors: n/a

Though somewhat drab, the white-fronted pionus is a great pet.

Length: 9 to 12 inches

Weight: 240 to 280 grams

Life span: Up to 15 years

Good as single pet? Yes

Good talker? No

Good at learning tricks? No

Good cuddler? Yes

Apartment dweller or house pet? Both

Relative cost: Moderate

Good for first-time owners? Yes

Take note: The gentle nature of the pionus makes it a good pet for a home with children in it.

Psittacula Parakeets

Psittacula parakeets are slender, long-tailed birds that measure about 16 inches in length. One member of the family, the ring-necked parakeet, takes its name from a thin ring of feathers that rings the necks of mature birds. Other parakeets in this family include the plum-headed parakeet (males have vibrant purple head feathers), the slaty-headed parakeet (males have gray head feathers), and the moustached parakeet (the male has a band of dark feathers across the top of his beak). Most are bright green, but blue and lutino (yellow) mutations are available. In the wild, *Psittacula* are found in parts of Africa and Asia.

The personalities of the *Psittacula* parakeets range from the comical Indian ring-necked to the talkative plum-headed to the sweet slaty-headed. Some species are sexually dimorphic, which means the males and females look different, while others are not.

Psittacula can become quite good talkers, and they can learn to perform tricks. A male ring-neck I know, Larry Bird (so named because the Boston Celtics were in the NBA playoffs the year his owners got him), has a vocabulary of about 50 words. His repertoire includes "Wipeout!" (he is, after all, a California bird) and "Here Kitty, Kitty," which he uses to call the cats he shares his home with.

These active parrots need large cages because they need ample room for their long tail feathers and because they need space in which to exercise. The cage should be at least 18 by 18 by 24 inches with bar spacing between $^1/_2$ to $^3/_4$ inches.

Psittacula also enjoy spending time out of their cages with their owners. Some birds may bond with only one member of the family, while others can be handled by all family members with equal ease. *Psittacula* should be fed pellets supplemented with fresh fruits and vegetables, such as corn on the cob, carrots, peas, and cooked beans. With good care, psittacula can live 20 years or more.

At a Glance

Common name: *Psittacula*

Scientific name: *Psittacula eupatria* (Alexandrine parakeet), *P. krameri* (Indian, African, or rose-ringed parakeet), *P. himalayana* (slaty-headed parakeet), *P. cyanocephala* (plum-headed parakeet), *P. roseata* (blossom-headed parakeet), *P. derbiana* (Derbyan parakeet), and *P. alexandri* (moustached parakeet).

Other names: n/a

Native habitat: *Psittacula* are found in deciduous forest, well-wooded country, cultivated farmland, parks, gardens, and coconut plantations across a wide range of Asia and Africa.

Common color: Green

The derbyan, a parakeet with pizzazz.

Noted for its talking potential, the plum-headed parakeet.

Other colors: Blue, lutino, albino, gray, pied, turquoise, and cinnamon

Length: 15 to 20 inches

Weight: 105 to 115 grams

Life span: Up to 25 years

Good as single pet? Yes

Good talker? Yes

Good at learning tricks? Yes

Good cuddler? Sometimes

Apartment dweller or house pet? Both

Relative cost: Moderate

Good for first-time owners? Yes

Take note: The *Psittacula's* ability to talk has been prized for thousands of years. Ancient Indian law prohibited the killing of these birds because their speaking talents were considered sacred by the Brahmins. Some Romans also taught their *Psittaculas* to greet the Emperor with "Hail, Caesar!"

Quaker Parakeets

Quaker or monk parakeets are small, saucy parrots from South America. They measure about 11 inches in length and come in a variety of colors, including green, cinnamon, lutino (yellow), and blue.

How these parrots got their names is a bit of a mystery. Several sources cite the similarity between the bird's green-and-gray plumage and a monk's habit as the reason why the bird is sometimes called the monk parakeet. The Quaker name may result from a shaking behavior seen in young birds about to be fed or from the birds' "Quakki" call in the wild.

Quakers are the only parrot species that build nests (other parrots are cavity nesters, finding holes in trees that they use to raise their young). One community-style Quaker nest found in the wild weighed more than 2,700 pounds and contained separate chambers for each pair of birds that lived in it.

Quakers can develop good vocabularies, but some people find their voices rather loud. They are also capable of learning to do tricks. They can also become accomplished escape artists, so be sure to house your pet in a secure cage. Some birds demonstrate pack rat tendencies, so don't be surprised to find a variety of small, shiny objects in your Quaker's cage that it has found around your home.

Quakers can be aggressive toward other birds and humans who invade their space. They can also become possessive of their favorite person in the home. Quakers are outlawed in some states because they are perceived as an agricultural threat if they escape. They aren't legal in my state, so I have no hands-on experience with them. Informed sources tell me that they are entertaining little parrots with big personalities.

Quakers should be housed in large cages and provided with plenty of toys because they love to chew. The minimum cage size for a Quaker would be 18 by 18 by 24 inches with $^1/_2$- to $^3/_4$-inch bar spacing. They also enjoy daily baths. They should be fed pellets, supplemented with fresh fruits and vegetables, such as carrots, zucchini, asparagus, cauliflower, and leafy greens. With good care, Quakers can live 25 to 30 years.

At a Glance

Common name: Quaker parakeet

Scientific name: *Myiopsitta monachus*

The Quaker parrot, a little bird with a big personality.

Other names: monk parakeet

Native habitat: Quakers are found in open forest, savannah woodlands, palm groves, orchards, and farmlands in South America. Feral colonies of escaped pet birds have become well-established in several US locations, including the Chicago area, Florida, Texas, Connecticut, Washington State, and New York.

Common color: Green

Other colors: Cinnamon, lutino, and blue

Length: 11 inches

Weight: 150 grams

Life span: Up to 30 years

Good as single pet? Yes

Good talker? Yes

Good at learning tricks? Yes

Good cuddler? Sometimes

Apartment dweller or house pet? Both

Relative cost: Moderate

Good for first-time owners? Yes

Take note: Some states prohibit Quaker ownership because of a long-standing fear that escaped pet birds might pose a threat to agriculture. As of the time of publication, these states had restrictions on Quaker ownership: California, Connecticut, Georgia, Hawaii, Kansas, Kentucky, Maine, Missouri, New Hampshire, New Jersey, New York, Ohio,

Pennsylvania, Rhode Island, Tennessee, Vermont, Virginia, and Wyoming. Check with your state Department of Agriculture to ensure that Quakers are legal in your state before adopting one.

Senegals

Senegals are one of the more popularly kept members of the *Poicephalus* family of parrots, which also includes the Meyer's (*Poicephalus meyeri*), the Jardine's (*P. gulielmi*), and the red-bellied parrot (*P. rufiventris*). Senegals are 9-inch-tall green, gray, and orange African parrots that may learn to talk and to perform tricks.

The *Poicephalus* family of parrots contains some hidden gems. Again, some people overlook these birds because they may not be as eye-catching as other, more brightly colored parrots. As a rule, *Poicephalus* parrots are good around children, can entertain themselves while their owners are away from home (if the birds are provided with an ample supply of toys and other safe diversions) and they are loving, playful pets. Some people consider the voices of these small parrots rather shrill, so listen closely and think carefully before adopting a Senegal.

The Senegal is a small, clever, and active parrot.

Senegals should be housed in medium-sized cages, and they should be given plenty of toys that they can chew on and destroy. The minimum cage size for a Senegal would be 18 by 18 by 24 inches with ½- to ¾-inch bar spacing. Their diet should include pellets supplemented with fresh foods, such as oranges, bananas, peas, spinach, corn, and apples. With good care, Senegals can live 15 years or more.

At a Glance

Common name: Senegal parrot

Scientific name: *Poicephalus senegalus*

Part 1

Closely related to the Senegal, the red-bellied parrot.

Other names: n/a

Native habitat: Senegal parrots live in savannah woodland and open forests in central-western Africa.

Common color: Gray, green, orange, and yellow

Other colors: n/a

Length: 9 inches

Weight: 125 to 150 grams

Life span: Up to 50 years

Good as single pet? Yes

Good talker? No

Good at learning tricks? Sometimes

Good cuddler? Sometimes

Apartment dweller or house pet? Apartment

Relative cost: Moderate

Good for first-time owners? Yes

Take note: In the *Poicephalus* family of parrots, only the red-bellied parrot and the Ruppell's parrot are sexually dimorphic. Male red-bellied parrots are more brightly colored than females, and female Ruppell's are more brightly colored than males. The Ruppell's is not commonly available in the pet trade.

The Aviary Birds

These species can be kept as single pets in the home, but they also suitable for life in an outdoor aviary:

Cockatiels

Finches

Kakarikis

Lovebirds

Neophemas

Parakeets

Rosellas

Aviary Birds

Information about parakeets, cockatiels, and lovebirds is provided in the main text, so let's look now at the care requirements of the kakariki, the neophema, and the rosella.

Kakarikis (*Cyanoramphus* species) hail from New Zealand. They weigh about 100 grams and measure about 9 inches in length. Their name comes from a Maori word for "little parrot." These highly active, mostly green birds make bold, curious additions to an aviary. They have been called the "Sherlock Holmes of the parrot world" because they investigate their environment so thoroughly.

Two species–the yellow crowned and the red fronted–are available in the United States. The species take their name from small patches of either yellow or red feathers that appear on the birds' heads or foreheads. These birds are moderately priced.

The active Bourke's parakeet is best suited to aviary life.

Kakarikis are persistent chewers, so make sure to supply these birds with an ample supply of chewable toys and perches. Their high activity level gives them a good appetite, so be sure to provide plenty of pellets supplemented with broccoli, grapes, kiwi, carrots, oranges, corn, cooked beans, well-cooked eggs, or mealworms.

Neophema parakeets include the Bourke's (*N. bourkii*), the turquoisine (*N. puchella*), and the elegant (*N. elegans*). These Australian natives weigh about 55 grams and measure about 7 inches in length. They come in a variety of colors and are gentle, quiet birds. They are noted for their whistling ability and the sweet sound of their voices.

Unlike the other birds described in this section, *Neophemas* can be kept as pets. They enjoy human companionship and are well suited for apartment living because of their small voices. However, these birds have a regular need for the type of exercise that only life in

Rosellas, which love to fly, do best in an aviary or flight.

an aviary can provide, which is why I've included them in this section.

Neophemas are moderately priced. Their diet includes pellets supplemented with seeds such as millet, flax, and rape seed; fresh greens such as spinach or beet tops; carrots; broccoli; corn; cooked beans and rice; and well-cooked eggs.

Rosellas (*Platycercus* species) are native to Australia. They are 10 to 14 inches long and weigh between 180 and 200 grams. They can be somewhat aggressive, so take care when adding these birds to an existing aviary collection.

Rosellas need a lot of room to fly, which is one reason they're ideal for aviary living. Another characteristic that makes them suitable for aviary living is the fact that they dislike cuddling and other close interaction with people. Rosellas also like to chew, so provide lots of wooden toys and perches in the aviary for them to destroy. Rosellas are also well-known for their whistling ability. They are moderately priced.

Diet requirements include pellets supplemented with fresh foods. Some species enjoy occasional treats of live food, such as insects or mealworms. Commonly kept varieties include the eastern, the western, and the crimson.

Going Home

This is a very exciting time for you—your bird will be coming home soon! To make the transition into your home as stress-free as possible on your pet, you'll need to have made sure your house is as safe as possible and that all family members are ready for your bird to be part of your home.

Although it may seem like I'm putting the cart before the horse, now is also a good time to locate an avian veterinarian who will care for your feathered friend. It's a good idea to select an avian veterinarian before you bring home your bird in case you want to have the bird examined on your way home from the bird store, breeder, or airport. Some stores and breeders offer limited warranties on their birds, and many

Treats may help build trust.

"Step up" is the most important command for handling a bird.

require a veterinary exam shortly after purchase in order for the warranty to be valid.

Bird-Handling Basics

One of the first things you'll need to know when you get your pet home is how to handle it. The pet store staff or breeder will likely review these steps with you, but it's easy to forget a step or two when it's just you and your bird alone for the first time. So let's review the basics of handling your bird:

Although some birds, including finches and canaries, would prefer not to be handled, the "up" and "down" commands will offer a great deal of control over many parrot. To teach the "up" command, simply have it step onto a stick or onto your hand while saying "Step up." You may want to gently press your hand or the stick against your bird's belly as you say "Up." Your bird will likely step up onto your hand or the stick without much additional encouragement, and it will soon respond to the command without you having to press the stick or your hand into its belly.

As you're teaching the "up" command, teach the "down" command, too. Simply say "Down" as you put the bird on its cage or playgym. These two commands provide you with a great deal of control over your bird because you can use them as discipline methods.

When handling your pet parrot for the first time, you may wish to use a towel to protect your hands from your bird's beak. Veterinarians and groomers frequently towel birds before handling them because a toweled parrot is often easier to control than an untoweled one.

To "towel" your bird, first drape the towel loosely over your hand. Turn the towel on a diagonal so that it looks like a diamond before draping it over your hand, and allow two-thirds of the diamond to fall below your hand. This is the part that you will wrap around your bird's body, while the other one-third will be wrapped around the bird's head.

Once you have the towel in place, reach into your bird's cage and catch it behind its head with your toweled hand. Move decisively and quickly because hesitation can give your bird a chance to strike at you and perhaps even bite. Lift the bird out of its cage and wrap its body in the towel as you bring the bird out of its cage. Be sure not to constrict your bird's chest as you hold it or carry it while it's toweled. Birds don't have diaphragms as we do, so they need to be able to expand and contract their chest muscles freely in order to breathe.

One of the most important parts of toweling a bird is being sure to use a towel that's sized to fit your bird. A parakeet will just get lost in a bath towel, and a washcloth won't offer you any protection from a large macaw.

Bird-Proofing Your Home

Bird-proofing your home means taking precautions to protect your bird from injuring itself. If you have children, you already know the concept of baby-proofing to protect infants and toddlers from harm as they explore their surroundings. The idea is similar: to protect a curious bird from hurting itself in your home.

Look at your home from your bird's point of view. What looks tempting? What interests you most? What could be harmful?

Before you bring your bird home, go through your house carefully. Perhaps work in just one room a day, and make sure it's as safe as it can be. Remove tempting or interesting items that could harm your pet. Cover power cords with PVC pipe or other protective sleeves to prevent your pet from chewing on them. Make sure your windows and doors are all securely screened to protect against unexpected escapes when your bird is out of its cage. Cover mirrors to keep your pet from flying into them, and consider putting stickers on your patio door to let your bird know that a large piece of glass is there. Take steps to make mini-blind or drapery pulls safer so your bird isn't strangled by them, and

Toweling may protect both you and your bird from harm.

remember not to run your ceiling fan while your pet is out of its cage. By taking a few common sense precautions, you can make your home a safe, happy place for your bird!

Room By Room: Household Hazards To Your Bird

Bathroom: open toilet, cosmetic or cleaning product fumes, prescription/nonprescription medications

Bedroom: pillows, candles, vases full of water, jewelry, cosmetic fumes

Don't Do It

If you can smell a household product, don't use it around your bird.

Kitchen: uncovered trash cans, open appliances, hot toasters or stove elements, covered pots on the stove, unsafe foods, household chemicals, overheated nonstick cookware, glasses full of liquid, decorative ceramicware treated with a lead glaze

Living room: furniture cushions, toxic houseplants, fireplace matches, full ashtrays, leaded glass suncatchers or lampshades, vases full of water

Home office: computer cords, pens, markers, staplers, pushpins, scissors, laminators, toner cartridges

Garage/Basement: hot glue guns, paints, solvents, glues, hand or power tools, car cleaning and maintenance products, fertilizer, insecticides, other gardening products

One odorless but deadly fume that may occur in your home is carbon monoxide. To protect your health as well as your bird's, scrupulously maintain your furnace, oven, stove, and other appliances that use fossil fuels such as natural gas. Contact your local utility company to find out if it offers free appliance checks for carbon monoxide. If you start developing flulike symptoms or find yourself suffering from a constant headache or nausea, have a qualified technician check your appliances for possible carbon monoxide emissions.

Bird-proofing can prevent a number of mishaps and injuries.

Other Safety Tips

In addition to bird-proofing your home, you can take other steps to ensure your pet bird's safety. One of the most important things you can do is make sure your bird's wings are clipped (with the exception of finches and canaries). A step-by-step explanation of wing clipping appears in Chapter 8. By keeping your bird's wings clipped, you protect it from harm and also prevent accidental escapes.

Another step you can take to protect your pet is to have it permanently identified. Because pet birds don't routinely wear collars, bird owners rely on either tattoos or microchips to identify their pets. Either method provides a permanent record of ownership in case your bird is lost or stolen.

Hidden Hazards: Fumes

Many fumes found in your home may be harmful to your bird's health. These include cleaning products, cigarettes, incense, potpourri, and overheated nonstick cookware. A good rule of thumb to follow is if you can smell it, don't use it around your bird. If you must use scented products around your bird, do so cautiously, and open windows immediately after using the product to air out your home.

Fitting in the Feathers

This next section is designed for parents with children and for potential bird owners who have other pets and want to know how to help a bird fit comfortably into their existing families.

Birds and Children

Birds can make very good pets for children, provided that parents are willing to help their children care for the bird. Bird ownership can teach children how to be kind and gentle toward animals, and it can also help foster a respect for nature. In some cases, birds have helped calm hyperactive children or have given seriously ill children something positive to focus on to take their mind off health issues.

Before you and your child take on the responsibility of bird ownership, shop around. Learn which types of bird interest your child, and encourage him or her to learn more about the bird of choice. By visiting bird stores in your area and by reading more about a particular type of

Closely supervise interactions between birds and children.

bird, your child will find out whether or not he or she is really ready for bird ownership, and you will be able to gauge if your child's interest wanes or remains high.

Explain to your child that daily care is an important part of bird ownership, and review the daily care steps from this book with him or her. Also tell your child about other care requirements, such as weekend cage cleaning, routine grooming, and regular veterinary visits, that a pet bird needs to remain healthy. Finally, remind your child about some basics of bird etiquette, such as not poking at the bird with fingers, not teasing the bird, and not feeding the bird anything without checking with you or another adult who is knowledgeable about bird care.

> **Best Birds for Children**
> * parakeets
> * cockatiels
> * conures
> * parrotlets
> * ring-necked parakeets

The best birds for children include parakeets, cockatiels, conures, parrotlets, and ring-necked parakeets. All of these are small- to medium-size birds, which are easier for children to handle than the large species. None of the species named above have a reputation for being aggressive or overly nippy.

Cats can learn to get along well with birds, but keep a watchful eye on them.

As you and your child prepare to become bird owners, remind him or her to be quiet around the bird and its cage, to not shake the bird's cage or poke at it, and to not take the bird (with or without its cage) outside without your permission.

Birds and Other Pets

Supervision is the key to ensuring domestic tranquility if you're trying to add a bird to a multiple-pet home. Birds can be successfully added to a home with other pets, but bird owners must be willing to take responsibility for the well-being of all their animal friends.

First of all, if you already have birds in your home, you'll have to quarantine the new arrival for at least 30 days to ensure the health of all your birds. By quarantine, I mean that the newest bird in your home will have to be housed in a separate part of your house, far away from your other birds. You'll need to feed and play with your newest pet bird after you feed and play with your other birds, and make sure that you change clothes and wash your hands thoroughly after handling your new bird or its utensils and before handling other birds in your home. All these quarantine measures are designed to prevent any hidden diseases from spreading from your new bird to your other feathered friends, so make sure to follow them carefully. Check with your avian veterinarian to find out how long your new bird will need to be quarantined.

Although you may automatically assume cats and birds won't cohabitate well, they can learn to get along. One set of friends I used to bird-sit had a house that included three cats, two birds, and a retired racing greyhound. Although the greyhound went to the kennel when these friends traveled, the cats and the birds stayed home. I took care of the birds and another friend tended to the needs of the cats.

Some cats may eagerly watch the quick movements of smaller birds, such as canaries, lovebirds, cockatiels, parrotlets, or parakeets, and the cat is likely to consider such small birds as prey. Never allow your cat and your smaller birds to be alone together and all should be well in your animal kingdom. Cats may be less likely to bother larger species, such as macaws, African greys, or cockatoos, but why tempt fate? A cat's claws and mouth contain bacteria that are extremely harmful to your pet bird, so don't give your cat the opportunity to claw or bite your pet bird, even accidentally.

Don't assume that just because your cat doesn't seem interested in your birds that all is well. When I worked at *Bird Talk*, we had a cat, Molly, who was the office's mascot. Molly oversaw the comings and goings of a veritable zoo between the dogs, cats, and birds that came in for photo shoots or to visit the office with their owners. We also had a parakeet that lived in the office from Monday morning to Friday night. He spent the weekends at his owner's townhome, but spent

Free time out of the cage is a treat in itself.

the week in the office because she worked long hours. Most of the birds didn't even cause Molly to twitch a whisker, but she quickly became interested in a Pacific parrotlet that fluttered off its owner's desk and onto the floor. Molly must have thought it was raining birds, and she started to stalk. Suddenly, our slow-moving mascot was ready for action. Only a loud shout and some quick movements on the part of the parrotlet's owner to distract Molly's attention from the bird kept it from becoming a morsel for Molly.

Dogs and pet birds usually get along well together, but owners have to make sure that the bird isn't injured by being sat on or stepped on by a large dog. Some hunting dogs may not do as well with pet birds, but most breeds do well with birds if owners are willing to supervise all interactions.

Less information is available about how birds fare in homes with small exotic mammals and reptiles. Some bird experts believe ferrets cannot overcome their highly developed hunting instinct, which makes them unsuitable companions for birds. Watch your pet bird around large reptiles because some species may consider your pet bird to be fair game.

If your pet bird is injured by another pet in your home, contact your avian veterinarian immediately because your pet may need emergency treatment (for bacterial infection from a bite or scratch, or for shock from being stepped or sat on) to save its life.

An avian vet is best qualified to care for your bird's health.

Selecting a Veterinarian

Although it may seem premature to select a veterinarian before you select a bird, it's actually a good idea to have a doctor available to examine your bird before you bring it home and to answer any questions you may have as a new bird owner. Avian veterinarians can provide bird owners with up-to-date information on avian medicine, nutrition, and general bird care. Their offices also can provide behavioral counseling, bird boarding, bird grooming, and other important services for birds and their owners.

To locate an avian veterinarian in your area, ask the person you're buying your bird from to make a recommendation. Ask other bird owners you know which veterinarian they use. You can also check advertisements in your local yellow pages for veterinary hospitals that specialize in birds. Such hospitals may be affiliated with the Association of Avian Veterinarians or they may advertise that they have an avian specialist on staff.

After you've found some likely candidates, call the veterinary offices. Find out how many birds the hospital staff examines each month, how much an office visit costs, and what payment options are available. Make an appointment for your bird to be evaluated if you like the answers you receive, and start to make a list of questions to ask the doctor. These can include what makes up a good bird diet, how often your pet needs to have its nails and wings trimmed, or how often the bird should be checked by the hospital staff.

Before the Bird Comes Home

- Become familiar with how to safely handle your bird.
- Bird-proof your home.
- Discuss the bird's arrival with your children. Determine how you'll fit the bird into your home if other pets are present. Plan to supervise all interactions between bird and children or pets.
- Find an avian veterinarian and set up a first-time examination for your bird.
- Set up the bird's cage and other accessories.

Homecoming Day

Now that you've set up the cage and become familiar with the daily and weekly care requirements, it's time to bring your bird home. You'll need to take your travel carrier with you to the pet store or breeder's house. In addition to your bird, you're likely to bring home a supply of food that's familiar to your bird, some basic care handouts, and maybe even a toy or two.

Even with clipped wings, a pet bird is in danger outside.

Getting Acquainted: The First Week with Your Bird

Give your new bird a few days to settle into its new environment after you bring it home. Don't spend all your time playing with your new pet outside its cage. If you do this, your bird will become accustomed to constant handling, which may confuse it later on when

Canaries need to adjust to a new home before singing again.

the novelty of being a bird owner has worn off a bit for you and you don't spend every waking moment with your pet.

Try to set up a realistic schedule that includes time for your bird inside its cage as well as time with you and the rest of your family so your bird will know that it will have periods during the day when it will have to entertain itself. Make sure to provide a variety of interesting toys in your pet's cage, and leave a radio or television on if you will be away from home for long periods of time. When you're moving around your bird's cage, talk softly to your pet and move slowly to avoid startling it.

Although it sounds difficult to do, allowing your bird to settle into your home's routine before bringing a lot of guests over to see your new pet is really a good idea. In my case, I gave my bird about two weeks to settle into my household routine before I exposed her to new people. I fed her and changed her water bowl twice a day and cleaned out her cage. I talked to her as I did all these things and told her what a good bird she was. As much as I wanted to show her off to my friends, she'd been through a great deal and I thought it was better to wait.

I knew we were on the right track when I heard a small voice that sounded very much like my own ask "Do you want to come out?" one night as I was washing the dinner dishes. I went into the living room and found my bird sitting in the doorway of her cage, talking quietly to herself. When she saw me in the living room, she asked me (again in my voice) "Do you want to come out?"

Soon after, I began introducing new people into her environment. They all treated her with respect and spoke softly around her. They didn't make any threatening movements around her and allowed her to get to know them on her terms. Within a few months, she was comfortable around my family and friends.

Soon after your pet comes home, it will be doing what normal, healthy birds do during the day–eating, playing, sleeping, and preening. By observing your bird each day, you will soon recognize its usual routine. Your pet may fluff its feathers to greet you or greet you with a special chirp or even a "hello" when you uncover its cage in the morning.

As a new bird owner, you may panic the first time you see your pet asleep. Some birds tuck their heads under their wings, while others rest on one foot during naptime. Still others, especially conures, sleep in their food bowls on their backs and appear dead while taking a nap. All these positions may be normal sleeping positions, so be aware of what is normal for your pet during its naptime.

Your bird will often rest with one foot tucked up into its belly feathers. If your bird consistently perches with both feet, however, or if your bird spends all its time on the cage floor, make an appointment for your pet to be seen by your avian veterinarian because it may be ill and unable to perch normally.

Give your bird time to adjust to life in your home. Parrots are long-lived birds, so it's possible your pet could be part of your life for many years to come, so there's no need to rush the first few days or weeks together. By allowing your pet to settle in to your home on its terms, you will show your bird that you are a trustworthy creature, which will go a long way toward building a strong relationship with your pet.

Relax, it's time to cuddle.

As Your Bird Settles In

• Have realistic expectations as your bird settles into your home's routine. For instance, don't invite the whole neighborhood in to see the bird during its first week in your home.

• Be sensitive to your bird's needs during the adjustment period.

• Move slowly around your bird at first, and speak quietly to it in order to get it accustomed to your voice and movements.

Happy Homemaking

Bringing a bird into your home means more than just having your feathered friend around. With your bird will come a cage, a playgym, and other accessories–all of which will need cleaning and regular maintenance in order to keep your bird healthy and happy.

In this chapter, we'll look at the type of cage that is best suited for your parrot. A bird's home needs to be spacious, secure, and clean. It should also be well stocked with safe toys and other accessories. We'll look at accessories such as bowls, perches, toys, and playgyms that your bird needs to maintain its physical and mental health. We'll discuss the aviary option for those bird owners who have the desire and the outdoor space to build a special

Bigger is better when it comes to cages.

place for their birds. We'll also look at what's involved in a bird's daily, weekly, and annual care routine.

Choosing a Cage

Over the years, birdcages have evolved from elaborate, highly intricate structures that really didn't provide a lot of useful space for the bird that lived inside to functional living spaces that are also attractive.

In the past, birdcages were made of either wood or metal wire. The wooden cages were designed for canaries, finches, or songbirds, while the wire cages were created to house parrots. If you're offered an old wooden cage for your parrot, tactfully turn down the offer. Wooden cages are difficult to clean and disinfect completely, and your parrot can easily chew a hole through the side because the wooden cage parts aren't designed to stand up to a parrot's chewing abilities.

Shade is critical whenever a bird is outside.

To combat seed hulls and other bird-related debris, the Duchess of Devonshire commissioned a canary cage made completely of glass. The cage's floor, roof, and water bowl were made of Waterford crystal that was inset into a burnished steel rim that helped hold the glass side and end pieces in place. The roof was a louvered canopy that could be opened so the duchess could hear her birds sing. Cage cleaning was made easier with a slide-out bottom. Cage manufacturers revisited this design idea in the mid-1990s when several companies created acrylic cages for smaller parrots, canaries, and songbirds. These cages were practical in terms of keeping bird debris in the cage, but they never quite caught on with bird owners.

Although you may be tempted to purchase an antique wire cage to house your pet, please resist this temptation. It's often difficult to determine the type of metal used to create these cages, and your bird could be poisoned or injured by chewing on the wires. Birds can also trap toes, wing tips, or beaks in some of the intricate nooks and crannies found on these older cages. Old birdcages are really better suited to house the stuffed birds or potted plants they now hold in many antique malls than they ever were as homes for pet birds.

When selecting a cage for your pet, don't forget that your bird won't be the only thing in the cage. You'll also have to allow room for a few perches, some toys, food and water bowls, and possibly a swing. However, don't overfill the cage because your pet will need room to climb, stretch, and flap its wings in order to exercise.

The first rule of birdcage buying is to purchase the largest cage you can afford in order to provide a spacious home for your pet. For smaller birds, long rectangular cages are preferred to tall, tubular styles because birds can get exercise flying from end to end, rather than being forced to sit on their perches only. For larger birds, purchase a cage that is at least large enough to let your pet stretch and flap its wings comfortably. Also remember to allow room for long tail feathers or crest feathers if your bird has one or both. A good rule of thumb to keep in mind is that the cage should be at least two times the bird's wing span in width and three times its length in height.

Make sure the cage you select is strong and durable. Check the finish carefully for chips and bubbles because some birds are quite determined chewers. Such birds will chew on weak spots in the cage finish, which can cause the bird to become ill and to make the cage look old and worn.

Check the bar spacing on the cage you select. Is it of an appropriate size for the bird you plan to keep in it? If you have any questions about the bar spacing of the cage you've chosen, ask a pet store employee or customer service representative of the company you're ordering

Rule of Thumb
Your bird's cage should be at least twice its wingspan in width and three times its length in height.

Cage elements such as bar spacing and direction are important.

Bar Spacing Recommendations

Veterinarian Gary Gallerstein recommends the following bar spacing for commonly kept pet birds:

- parakeets and lovebirds, $3/8$ inch
- cockatiels and small conures, $1/2$ to $3/4$ inch
- Amazons, African greys, and other medium-size parrots, $3/4$ to 1 inch
- macaws and large cockatoos, $3/4$ to $1^1/2$ inch
- canaries and finches, $3/8$ to $7/16$ inch

from. They should be able to direct you to appropriate cages for your bird. Also make sure the cage you choose has both horizontal and vertical bars to make climbing easier for your pet.

After you've evaluated the cage's quality and the spacing of the cage bars, check the cage door. The ideal door should be wide enough to let you get your bird in and out of the cage easily, and it should allow for easy movement of food and water bowls in and out of the cage, along with birdie bathtubs and other accessories. Another consideration for the door is that it locks securely enough to keep your bird in its cage, yet it is easy enough for you to operate.

The next item to check is the cage tray. Make sure the tray on the cage you select slides in and out easily because you will be changing the paper in this cage at least once a day for the rest of your bird's life. Pay attention to the shape of the tray. Will newspaper or clean paper towels fit into it easily, or will you need to cut paper into an unusual shape to line the tray? Experienced bird owners will tell you that the easier the tray is to clean, the more likely it will be cleaned each day.

Examine the cage floor to ensure it has a grille between the cage and the tray that will keep the bird out of the debris that falls into the tray. Having a grille helps ensure a pet bird's health because the bird does not have access to discarded food or its droppings, and a grille also helps keep the bird in its cage while the tray is being cleaned.

To Cover or Not To Cover?

In addition to the cage, you may wish to purchase a cage cover for your pet. Some bird owners find that the cover helps settle their pets down for bed, while others find that a dark cover helps their birds sleep better, especially if lights are left on around the bird's cage after it has gone to bed.

If you choose to cover your bird's cage, you can use a specially made cage cover, or an old sheet, towel, or blanket can also work well. Whatever you choose to use, make sure the material is clean and free of holes.

Some birds chew on their cage covers, and the cover will need to be replaced when it has too many holes in it to be an effective cover. Replacing a well-chewed cover will also help keep your bird from becoming entangled in the cover or caught in a ragged clump of threads. Some birds have injured themselves quite severely by being caught in a holey cage cover, so help keep your pet safe from this hazard.

Other Cage Accessories

Just as furniture and accessories helped make your house your home, so it goes with your bird's cage. Your bird will require a few items, such as dishes, perches, and toys, to make its cage more comfortable and more homelike.

When selecting dishes for your pet, pick up several sets so that mealtime cleanups are quick and easy. Owners of smaller species, such as parakeets and parrotlets, need to buy only uncovered dishes because some smaller birds are often reluctant to stick their heads into hooded feeders to eat and may starve rather than eat from such dishes.

When choosing perches for your pet's cage, buy perches of different diameters or materials so your bird's feet won't get tired of standing on the same-size perch

Recommended Perch Diameters

1/2 inch for parakeets and parrotlets

5/8 inch for cockatiels

3/4 inch for small conures

1 inch for medium-sized parrots, such as Amazons, large conures, miniature macaws, small cockatoos, or African greys

2 inch or larger for large macaws and cockatoos

Rope perches are a softer alternative to wood or concrete.

of the same material day after day. Birds spend most of their lives standing, so preventing foot problems is an important part of bird ownership. Preventing problems is much easier than trying to cure them.

Select a perch that's the right size for your pet, and another that's slightly larger than the recommended size. Offering different perch diameters allows your bird's foot muscles to be exercised more fully than if it has only one perch diameter in its cage.

Popular perch choices include traditional wooden dowels, natural wooden branches, rope, and terra cotta or concrete. The natural wooden branches provide different perch diameters for a bird's feet. Rope perches give different diameters, too, along with a somewhat softer surface on which to perch. The terra cotta or concrete perches are often sold as grooming perches, and they offer an abrasive surface on which birds can groom their beaks. These perches may also help keep a bird's nails trimmed, although some bird owners have found that their birds' feet are injured by the use of abrasive perches. If you notice your bird favoring one foot or that its feet suddenly seem red and tender after introducing an abrasive perch, remove it from the cage because the bird may be overusing the perch and may injure itself.

Another product touted as a bird grooming aid is the sandpaper perch cover. These rough sleeves, which slip over a perch, don't do much to trim a bird's nails, but they can create sore feet that can leave your bird prone to infections and other foot problems. Please protect your pet from harm by not using sandpaper perch covers.

When you install your bird's perches in its cage, give your bird different levels on which to perch by placing the perches at different heights. Don't place the perches over food and water bowls.

The Playgym

Playgyms can be as simple or as elaborate as you want them to be. Some are basic cagetop models, while others can stand almost as tall as the ceiling in your bird room. By visiting bird stores in your area or by looking at magazines about bird care, you will see a wide variety of playgyms offered for sale. Depending upon your bird's activity level and your budget, you can select a complicated gym with a series of ladders, swings, perches, and toys, or you can purchase a simple T-stand that has a place for food and water bowls and an eyescrew or two from which you can hang toys. Some handy bird owners build custom-made playgyms suited especially to their birds' sizes and activity levels.

Choosing Fun, Safe Toys

Bird owners need to consider two important criteria when selecting toys for their pets. The first is whether or not the bird will enjoy playing with the toy, and the second is whether or not the toy is safe.

The fun factor in toy selection is something that many bird owners learn over time. Some birds enjoy trying new types of toys and are up for almost anything that their owners bring home from the pet store, while others find change stressful and prefer to stick with tried-and-true, familiar toys. Owners of such birds may find themselves replacing a worn-out toy with a carbon copy, while other toys go unnoticed in the cage. By trying different types of toys on your pet, you'll soon learn what its likes and dislikes are, which will make toy buying easier for you and more enjoyable for your pet.

Safety First

Bird owners need to pay attention when purchasing toys. Here are just a few things to be aware of when selecting a toy for your bird:

- brittle plastic toys can shatter easily, especially when a larger bird is playing with the toys

- lead-weighted toys can be cracked open to expose the dangerous lead

- chains with links may be loose enough to catch toenails or beaks

- ring toys may be too small for a bird to climb through safely

- jingle-type bells can trap toes, tongues, or beaks

Quick and Easy Toys

- nuts in the shell
- cardboard rolls from paper towels
- dried pasta strung on leather strips
- magazine subscription cards

Safety concerns for pet bird owners include selecting a toy that is properly sized for their pet. Parakeets won't do well with macaw-size toys and vice versa. Large toys can scare small birds, and large birds can injure themselves if they accidentally break a toy that's made for a smaller bird's less-powerful beak.

Sturdy wooden toys, vegetable-tanned leather toys, and rope toys—all in appropriate sizes—are safe, entertaining toy choices.

Offer a play gym for fun and a change of scenery.

Some birds enjoy playing with a new toy right away, while others have to get used to a new toy from afar before allowing it into their cage. If your bird needs a little extra time to adjust to a new toy, try leaving it just outside the cage for a few days before installing it. Unless I was replacing a toy with an exact duplicate, my bird often needed a few days to become accustomed to a new plaything, and this trick really seemed to help her.

Some toys don't require a trip to the pet store. Many birds enjoy chewing on the cardboard rolls from paper towels, while others enjoy shredding the subscription cards in many magazines. Some birds find raw nuts in the shell, such as walnuts, filberts, or almonds, to be challenging playthings. Still others enjoy chewing on dry cereal or pasta that has been strung on clean string or vegetable-tanned leather.

Location, Location, Location

Now that you know how to select a cage and other accessories for your bird, let's talk about where the cage will go in your home. Be sure to set up the cage before your bird comes home because it will be easier and less stressful for both you and the bird if you have a place to put your new pet as soon as you both get home. The bird won't have to wait in its travel carrier while you set up the cage, and it can get down to the business of becoming part of your family.

When selecting a spot for your bird's cage, choose a place that is active, not too noisy, safe, and well lit. You should put the cage in a spot that will include your pet in daily family activities, such as the living room or family room. You have to strike a balance between an area where your bird will feel included in your home's daily routine and a place that might seem like Grand Central Station at the height of the rush hour. Birds like some activity around them on a regular basis, but too much hustle and bustle may add stress to it's life, especially if it's just getting to know you and your family. Your bird will need some time to relax and sleep, and if its cage is placed in a noisy, highly active area, it may not be able to rest and relax properly.

My parrot's cage used to sit near a north-facing living room window that offered light but no direct sun in one apartment and in the dining room in another. In still another apartment, I placed her cage in the corner of the living room that intersected with the hallway that led to the bedroom and bath. In all instances, I placed the cage so she was part of the apartment's activities and could feel like she was the center of attention, which she was. In all cases, I made sure to set up her cage so that one solid wall was always behind her. She seemed more comfortable with a solid wall behind her because nothing could sneak up and surprise her from behind.

As far as safety goes, make sure the birdcage sits on a solid base to prevent it from being tipped over. If it is equipped with casters for easy movement, lock the wheels to keep the cage from rolling unexpectedly. Keep the cage out of the kitchen or bathroom because chemicals used in these rooms could produce fumes that are harmful to a pet bird. Birds can also injure themselves on hot stoves or ovens in the kitchen, which is a good reason to keep them out of this room.

Lighting is the final point to consider when setting up your bird's cage. Your bird should have access to light each day. If your home isn't light and open, ask your avian veterinarian if your bird would benefit from a supplemental light similar to the "grow lights" used over some houseplants. In your quest to give your bird light, be sure not to put the bird's cage directly in a window because the bird can quickly overheat if left in direct sunlight with no shade available.

The Aviary Option

If you live in a temperate climate and have some extra room on your property, you may want to consider an outdoor aviary for your pet bird. Your aviary should have an outdoor flight in which the birds will spend much of their time, a door between the flight and the shelter for your birds to use in case of bad weather, a sloped roof and guttering system that directs rain away from the flight, a mesh ceiling to deter predators

Don't forget the toys!

and vermin, brick footings to ensure a longer-lasting foundation, and a sloping concrete or paving-stone floor. The aviary will also need a safety porch to reduce the chances of aviary residents escaping from their homes.

As you start to plan your aviary, you'll need to answer a few questions: Will the aviary be indoor or outdoor? How many birds will you keep in it? Is your area subject to temperature extremes at different times of the year?

Before you build your aviary, make arrangements to visit bird breeders in your area. If you can't see the actual aviaries, ask to see photos of the facilities and find out what the breeders would recommend that you do and not do. Find out which materials and designs were successful for them and which features in their aviaries they plan to change as soon as they can. You'll obtain a wealth of information from these discussions. Another good first step is order catalogs from aviary supply companies because these will give you additional design ideas and also help you figure out how much your aviary may cost.

One of the first questions you'll need to answer is which species you're going to keep in your aviary. Deciding which species of birds you'll keep will help you determine the size of the finished structure, and it will also guide you in determining how the aviary will be laid out.

If a colony of pet birds is what you have in mind, pay attention to compatibility issues. Don't mix large and small birds in the aviary because the larger ones may bully their smaller neighbors. Some species are naturally pugnacious within their own size range, while others are more passive. You'll need to consider personality types when making your decisions on which species you'll keep in order to keep peace in your aviary.

As you're designing your aviary, keep the following factors in mind: location, size, building materials, furnishings and accessories, security and service features, and pest control.

The first consideration for your aviary site should be to find a level site in your yard. Working with a level site from the start will make construction easier, more affordable, and less time-consuming than having to flatten or fill a less-than-level location.

When considering the location of your aviary, one of your first concerns should be the proximity of the aviary to your neighbors' property. Aviary birds can and will be noisy at times, and the noise may try your neighbors' patience severely. Discuss your aviary plans with your neighbors early on to allow them to voice their concerns before they become complaints about noise to the authorities. Fences and hedges can sometimes be used to shield your neighbors from the sights and sounds of your aviary; consider incorporating them into your plan.

Another situation to keep in mind when siting your aviary is the potential for bird theft. Because they are often expensive and fairly easy to steal, birds may tempt thieves, so a location close to your home is preferable to one that is out of sight of your home on a rarely visited corner of your property. An aviary close to your house also allows you to enjoy watching your birds as you savor a morning cup of coffee before starting your day or as you wind down from a long day at the office.

When selecting the site for your aviary, you'll also need to keep in mind your plans for future aviaries. Will you expand your collection at some point, or will the aviary you build be sufficient for your needs for the foreseeable future? If you want to expand, it's best to pick a site for the first building that can accommodate your future plans.

Another aspect to consider is what's under the aviary site. Will you have to access sewer or water pipes or gas lines? If so, you may want to locate the aviary in another part of your yard. However, you'll want to have your aviary in a location that allows you to connect it easily to electrical, water, and sewer lines.

Convenient food cups make for easy care and cleaning.

Keep your aviary away from shade trees. Although you might think building your aviary under a tree is a good idea, experts advise otherwise. Trees attract wild birds that can eliminate into the aviary, creating the potential for passing diseases along to your birds. Trees also drip water into the aviary after a rainstorm, and trees can also harbor insects that could bedevil your birds during warm weather. At the same time, you'll need to keep the aviary site out of direct sun because birds are quite susceptible to heatstroke. You can avoid this problem by designing an area in each flight under which birds can hide from the elements, or you can select a site that has existing partial shade.

Site your aviary so that it is protected from storms and prevailing winds. If you are subject to storms that blow in from the west, for example, build your aviary on the east side of your property so your house can serve as a protective barrier from the full force of the storms. You can also use trees in containers as a windbreak, or you can install plastic panels on the vulnerable sides of your aviary.

The next issue to worry about is the finished size of the aviary. This will depend on several criteria: the amount of money you have to spend, the size of the aviary site, and the species you plan to keep in the aviary.

Small parrots, such as cockatiels or Senegals, do well in flights that are about 3 feet wide, 9 feet long and 6 to 8 feet high. Medium parrots, such as Amazons and African greys, need flights that measure 4 feet wide by 12 feet long by 6 to 8 feet high. Larger parrots, such as macaws, require a flight that measures about 6 feet wide by 16 feet long by 6 to 8 feet high. The height and width are as much a concession to owner comfort as they are for the birds; it's easier to work in an aviary that allows you to stand upright comfortably, and it's easier to clean a wider aviary than a narrow one. Many species like to have space to climb, fly, and play, so it's best to build the flights as large as you can.

In addition to the flights themselves, allow yourself storage space for food and supplies, an area for food preparation, and a clean-up area in your aviary design. You will also need to leave room for a double-doored safety porch to ensure aviary residents do not escape when you enter or exit the aviary.

Building materials are another factor to consider when designing your aviary. You will need welded wire mesh panels for the flights, a frame to hold the panels in place, and a structure to shelter the birds in inclement weather and for storage. Although wood is the most commonly used material for aviary frame construction, steel or PVC pipe, cinder block, brick or aluminum can also be utilized under certain conditions. (Some parrots kept in aluminum-framed aviaries have chewed on the aluminum and ingested small particles of the metal, which has caused the birds to pick their feathers.) Some companies offer aviary kits that contain wire panels and other components to put together an outdoor aviary. You may want to pursue this option if you aren't particularly handy, but many people enjoy customizing their aviary design to meet their needs.

Welded wire mesh is more durable than wire netting or chicken wire, and it comes in a variety of sizes and gauges. The normal range of gauges used to keep birds is between 20 and 12. Sixteen gauge works well for lovebirds and conures, while Amazons, African greys, and miniature macaws can be kept behind 14 gauge wire. Cockatoos, macaws, and highly destructive birds should be kept behind 12 gauge wire. The 12 gauge mesh comes in sheets, while the other gauges are available in rolls.

When calculating the amount of wire mesh you'll need, remember to allow enough welded wire mesh to double line the partitions between your breeding flights to protect your aviary residents from being injured by nippy neighbors. If you use galvanized wire mesh, you will want to treat the mesh with a solution of vinegar and water before turning your birds loose in the aviary. Some birds that have chewed on new galvanized wire have fallen victim to zinc poisoning or "new cage syndrome," which can be fatal.

If you choose to construct a wooden frame for your aviary, you will need to treat the wood with a preservative to keep it from rotting. However, many of these products can be harmful to birds, so allow the preservative to dry completely before letting your birds into the finished aviary. It's also a good idea to cover the wood with wire or tin sheeting to prevent birds from chewing on it.

Add a quality travel carrier to your list of supplies.

Regardless of the material you choose for the frame and walls, you should plan on pouring a concrete floor for your facility. Concrete is easily cleaned and disinfected, it discourages vermin and predators from digging their way into the aviary, and it keeps parrots from tunneling out through an earthen floor. Design the floor with a slight slope for easier drainage during cleanup.

Roofing material choices include wood, tile, or asphalt shingles. In cold climates, you may want to consider a double roof with 6 inches of space between the layers. This will help minimize extremes in temperature, especially if you add insulation between the layers.

Depending on whether you build an outdoor or indoor aviary, your furnishings and accessories will vary slightly. In both cases, perches, food and water bowls, and nest boxes will be needed by aviary residents. Birds kept indoors will benefit from the use of night lights, ionizers, full-spectrum lighting, and heaters or air conditioners, while outdoor birds will need a sun shade of some sort, heat lamps in times of extreme cold, and a mister system to cool them during hot days.

When it comes to security, make sure you have a way to protect your birds from theft, whether it's an alarm system on the aviary, padlocks on all aviary doors and gates leading into your property, motion-detection lights, razor wire on your fence, guard dogs, or some combination of all of the above.

For some birds, a cage cover ensures a good night's sleep.

In terms of service features, be certain you'll construct your aviary in an area that can be easily connected to electrical, water, and sewer lines. Design the flights so they can be easily cleaned and serviced—don't design in a lot of nooks and crannies, for example, that will catch seed hulls, feathers, and other debris, and make the flights of a comfortable height and width so that you won't be discouraged from going in to clean them. Put food and water stations and nest boxes on the same end of the flight so that you can offer fresh food and water and check the boxes at the same time with minimal disturbance to your breeding pairs. Don't place food and water stations under your birds' perches because birds will eliminate in their food and water bowls, and contaminated food can cause disease problems in your stock.

Pest control measures can include placing all food in metal trash cans with tight lids to discourage mice and rats, installing fine mesh on all exterior aviary panels in addition to the welded wire mesh to discourage mice and snakes from crawling through the mesh and into the aviary, and practicing scrupulous maintenance and cleanup to reduce the number of insects in the aviary. Other measures to take are to extend the wire mesh about a foot past the bottom of the aviary and then bend the mesh at a 45-degree angle away from the aviary, which will discourage animals from burrowing into the aviary, and installing a double roof to keep predatory birds and cats away from aviary residents.

Once you have your design worked out, take it back to the breeders you talked to and ask them for their opinions. They may see huge problems in your design that can help you avoid headaches later on, or you may give them some ideas for future construction in their own facilities. After you've finalized your design, check with your local planning department to find out if your property is zoned for an aviary and if any permits or other paperwork will be required before you begin building.

Basic Pet Bird Care

Now let's talk about the level of care your bird needs each day. Although they don't require daily walks or regular brushings, pet birds do have certain daily care requirements to maintain their physical and mental health. They include:

• A careful visual examination from you. Pay attention to any changes in the bird's physical appearance and activity level. If your bird's routine seems to have changed, observe it closely the rest of the day. If the bird doesn't resume its normal routine by the next day, make an appointment with your avian veterinarian to have your bird examined. Changes in the bird's routine may indicate an illness or injury that requires veterinary attention.

• A supply of clean, fresh water and fresh food at least once a day. After you've removed the food and

Fouled cage litter can harbor harmful germs and bacteria.

water dishes from your bird's cage, wash them with detergent and hot water and rinse them thoroughly. When you change the bowls, pay attention to how much food your bird has eaten and how much water it has drunk. If you see changes in the amount of food or water being consumed, tell your avian veterinarian about them, especially if you see other signs of illness or injury.

• A clean cage tray liner at least once a day. When you change the liner in your bird's cage tray, look at its droppings. If the color, number, or consistency of the droppings doesn't appear normal, contact your avian veterinarian's office because your bird may need to be evaluated.

• Regular attention from you and playtime away from its cage. This is one of the most enjoyable parts of owning a bird. Some birds enjoy learning tricks, while others are content to perch on the back of a chair as you work in your home office. Still others like to be scratched and cuddled as you watch television in the evening. You'll have to learn what your bird likes to do and make sure that it has a chance to spend time with you each day.

• A consistent bedtime. Birds are creatures of habit, and they require a great deal of sleep (at least nine hours a night). Some birds benefit from having their cages covered at bedtime. Although you might think the cover helps keep the cage warm, it really serves as more of a signal to the bird that it's time to settle in for the night.

Weekly Housecleaning

Your bird's cage will need to be thoroughly cleaned and disinfected weekly to help keep your pet healthy. Some birds may require cage cleaning more frequently, but a weekly cage cleaning is a good rule of thumb to follow.

A quick way to start cleaning the cage each week is to stand the empty cage in the shower and turn on the hot water for about five minutes. The force of the water and the steam helps loosen some of the stuck-on food. After the water has run for a few minutes, use an old toothbrush, a scrubber sponge or some fine-grade steel wool to remove any debris that's still clinging to the bars. Once the cage is completely clean, disinfect it with a bird-safe disinfectant. Your avian veterinarian or bird supply store staff should be able to recommend a safe, effective product. Read and follow all label instructions carefully when using the disinfectant.

Rinse the cage thoroughly and dry it completely before returning your bird and its accessories to the cage. Check perches, toys, and other accessories as you put them back in the cage, and replace any items that are worn or frayed to ensure your pet's health and safety. Providing your bird with a clean home and offering it fresh food and water served in clean dishes are very good ways to protect your pet from illness. However, it's easy to let your bird's cage get dirty and stay that way. I know, I've been there. But if you do a little cleanup in the morning as you feed your bird its breakfast and a little more in the evening when you feed your pet its supper, you'll find that cage cleanup doesn't end up being a chore that consumes a large part of your weekend.

Don't Do It!
Never neglect to clean your bird's cage thoroughly at least once a week—it could save your bird's life!

Annual Care Issues

During the course of a year, your bird will need to visit your avian veterinarian for its annual checkup. The bird will also molt, or lose its feathers, at some point in the year. Some species molt during the summer months, while other birds seem to be in a perpetual molt. Discuss what a normal molting pattern should be for your bird with your avian veterinarian. Be prepared for some mood changes in your pet during the molt. Some birds are a little grumpier during this time, while others seem to think the sun rises and sets on their owners because the birds need someone to help them preen their newly forming feathers. Gently offer to scratch the incoming feathers as they begin to break through their feather sheaths–your bird may appreciate the assistance in scratching some very hard-to-reach places!

Part Two
Caring for a Bird

"Want to hear about my frequent fliers program?"

5

An Insider's Look at Bird Behavior

Understanding how and why our pet birds behave the way they do is one of the most popular discussion topics for both new and experienced bird owners. But this was not always the case. Ten to twenty years ago, most pet bird owners didn't invest a lot of effort into understanding avian behavior. They were more concerned with keeping their pets healthy. This was because almost all pet birds at that time were wild-caught imports. Trappers often weren't able to capture the healthiest animals in the jungle, so the birds they caught usually had some sort of health problem—sort of a pre-existing condition, to borrow a phrase from the medical insurance world. These health problems could sometimes be life-threatening and usually required an investment

Birds, even those in cages, retain their wild instincts.

of time and money on the part of a pet bird owner to resolve them. Sometimes, the problems couldn't be completely solved, but they could be managed. However, successful management often meant more time and money was invested by the bird owner to keep the pet on a regular routine of medications and veterinary visits. Behavior issues such as screaming, fear biting, and feather picking were often seen in these wild-caught birds, but the resources frequently weren't available to resolve the problems.

Today's pet bird is a healthier individual than its wild-caught cousins because it is domestically raised by a breeder. These breeders have an interest in producing healthy animals because healthy animals are more likely to be sold than unhealthy ones. Breeders invest a lot financially and emotionally in their birds, so owners don't have to worry as much about purchasing a pet bird with a pre-existing health problem.

Avian veterinarians are also refocusing their efforts to meet the needs of today's captive-bred birds. They are learning as much as they can about avian behavior to help their clients understand how and why their birds do what they do. Some clinics also offer new-bird-owner classes that discuss common behaviors, while others offer behavioral counseling for owners whose birds have developed behavior problems.

Because the captive-bred birds are healthier and more accustomed to people than the wild-caught birds were, breeders, owners, and avian veterinarians can now focus on issues, such as behavior problems, that affect the quality of the relationship between bird and owner. Today's birds are also likely to live longer than their wild-caught counterparts because they are healthier and better cared for from the start. A healthy bird living out its normal life span in a pet home will be part of the family for between 20 and 80 years, depending on species. If a creature is going to spend several decades in an owner's home, it's best for both the animal and the owner if the owner understands as much as he or she can about that animal's behavior.

In this chapter, we'll discuss normal and abnormal behaviors, most of which apply primarily to the parrots. You'll learn what signs indicate illness, boredom, or stress in your pet. We'll look at the big four of birdie misbehavior—biting, screaming, chewing, and feather picking—and learn why a bird doesn't see these behaviors as "bad." We'll also discuss some steps you can take to resolve problem behaviors in your parrot.

Normal Flock Behavior

To understand why your parrot behaves the way it does as a pet, we need to look to the behavior of wild parrots in their native lands. Parrots can be found in the wild on the continents of North America, South America, Australia, Africa, and Asia, and on some islands in the Caribbean and the South Pacific.

Wherever you find them, parrots are likely to be living in a flock that can be as small as a few birds to as large as several hundred members. The flock starts the day by greeting the dawn with a variety of noises. The noises let members of the flock know that the group will be on the move shortly. Once the flock members are all awake, the birds begin their daylong search for food.

During the day, birds make more noise. These noises tell members of the flock that one or more members have found food or that something dangerous is in the area. The birds look for food all day long. They also play by themselves and with other members of the flock. They continue to make noise to let other flock members know about possible dangers or to tell other birds in the area where they are. At the end of the day, the flock gathers and heads to a suitable roosting spot. The cycle begins again the following morning.

Our pet parrots demonstrate some behaviors that are similar to those of their wild cousins. They eat and play, they call to other members of the household, and they make noise at sunrise and sunset. My bird used to have a sunset ritual that included slide whistle imitations and other noises. My sister described the bird's routine as "singing down the

> **Take Note**
>
> If the advice offered in this book runs counter to advice you've received from your avian veterinarian or an avian behavioral consultant, please follow that advice instead. Your avian veterinarian or behaviorist has the advantage of having seen your bird and taken a detailed history on your pet, so he or she can offer advice tailor-made to your bird's specific needs.

Without its flock, your pet will need your companionship.

Part 2

Include your bird in everyday activities.

Quick and Easy Exercises:

Wing flapping

Ball chasing

Perch hanging

Playgym climbing

sun," and she heard it frequently during evening phone calls.

These behaviors have bad news/good news connotations for bird owners. The bad news is that eating, playing, and noise making are all normal parrot behaviors that you won't be able to change greatly. The good news is you can usually find a way to quiet your parrot's noise level.

As you watch your pet during the day, you'll see that it moves around its cage frequently. All this movement echoes the daylong search for food that wild parrots experience each day. As your bird moves, it probably uses its beak as much as its feet. Parrots are very good at using their beaks to climb, reach, hold, bite, hang, eat, preen, or play, depending on what their current activities call for.

Your pet parrot won't have to spend much time searching for its food, so you'll need to give it some mealtime challenges to help it use up the energy that would be spent in the food search. Occasionally offer food in different forms. For instance, give your bird whole green beans or peas in the pod so that your pet has to work for its food a little bit. Corn on the cob sliced into bird-size wheels or clean pine cones filled with nuts or fresh vegetables can give your bird something to work on during mealtime. You can also give your bird nuts in the shell to challenge its mind as well as nourish its body.

Be sure to give your bird plenty of playtime. This will help it burn off excess energy and will keep it from misbehaving. Birds that have active schedules become better companions than bored birds with time on their wings. Make sure your bird has plenty of safe, appropriate toys with which to play, and switch the toys in its cage regularly to prevent birdie boredom.

In addition to playing with toys, your parrot needs other exercise opportunities. These can include wing flapping, hanging from a perch, climbing on a playgym, or chasing a ball. Because each parrot's taste differs, you will have to try different activities to see which one is most interesting to your pet.

In addition to making sure your bird has toys to play with and regular exercise, make sure it gets to spend some quality fun time with you. You are part of your parrot's flock, so it's natural that you would play together. Some of the ways you can spend playtime with your parrot include tickling it, playing tug-of-war with it using a rope toy or cardboard paper towel roll, or encouraging it to exercise by gently raising and lowering your arm while your bird perches on it and flaps.

Normal Captive Parrot Behavior

So just what is normal parrot behavior? Well, normal parrot behavior depends a lot on the species of bird you're keeping and its individual personality. Some birds like to show off, while others tend to be shy, so you'll have to learn what is normal for your bird's species as well as its personal idiosyncrasies.

Typically, normal parrot behavior involves a lot of playing, climbing, and wing flapping. Healthy, normal parrots play with toys and with the food in their food bowls. They chew a lot to keep their beaks in condition and to help them burn off energy. They preen their feathers frequently during the day, putting a lot of time and effort into cleaning and straightening each one. Some parrots enjoy a daily or weekly bath, while others aren't particularly interested in bathing.

Normal parrots vocalize throughout the day. They are often noisiest early in the morning and at dusk, which echoes wild parrot behavior that calls the flock together in the morning to go forage for food and again at night when the birds are ready to go to sleep.

Naps and restful periods are perfectly normal for birds.

Normal parrots also nap during the day. Some birds take frequent short naps, while others have definite nap periods in the afternoon. Some birds find it perfectly normal to sleep on the floor of their cages with their feet in the air, or they nod off on their backs in their food bowls. Learn where your bird likes to sleep and in what position, and be sure to warn anyone who takes care of your bird that it likes to sleep in strange positions so that person isn't alarmed if the bird ends up on the cage floor and appears to be seriously ill or dead.

Behaviors That Indicate Illness

Birds show signs of illness in very subtle ways. This is a holdover from their wild beginnings because birds that act sick in the wild are often taken advantage of by predators. By the time a pet looks or acts as if it is sick, it is really seriously ill, so it's important for owners to recognize signs of illness quickly and take the bird for an examination by an avian veterinarian.

Here are some signs of illness to watch for:

• bird sits with its feathers fluffed all the time

• bird has lost its appetite

• bird seems to sleep all the time

• bird doesn't seem to be eliminating in a normal pattern

• bird's dropping have suddenly changed color or consistency

• bird has lost weight

• bird has lost interest in daily activities

• bird cannot hold up its wings

• bird becomes lame

• bird has partially eaten food stuck to its face

• bird has regurgitated food onto the cage floor

• bird's breathing is labored (with or without tail bobbing)

• bird has runny eyes or nose

• bird stops vocalizing

If you notice any of these signs of illness in your pet, contact your veterinarian's office immediately for further instructions. Your bird should be seen as soon as possible to rule out any illnesses.

Bored Bird Behaviors

A pet parrot may become bored because its owners don't offer it enough to do. Because parrots are very intelligent animals, they need mental challenges to keep their lives interesting, and if they don't receive them, they become bored. Parrots can demonstrate that they are bored in a number of ways. They can pick their feathers, shred paper, scream, chew on items they shouldn't, become overly fussy eaters, or simply overeat. None of these situations is healthy for a parrot, and most can be easily prevented.

The first step to take to prevent boredom in your pet bird is to make sure it feels like it's part of your family. Place your bird's cage in a room of the house that you spend time in each day, such as the family room or a home office if you're lucky enough to be able to work at home. Although breeding birds may need privacy and some peace and quiet to successfully raise chicks, single pet birds need to be included in your daily routine to keep them mentally healthy.

Free time is a good time for some vigorous wing flapping.

Another simple step you can take to prevent your bird from becoming bored is to rotate the toys in its cage regularly. Check the toys for signs of wear when you're changing them, and replace any that have well-worn parts that your bird could injure itself on. Notice which types of toys your bird enjoys playing with and which ones get ignored so you'll know which types to purchase in the future.

Make sure to spend a little time each day with your pet, too. If your pet enjoys having its head scratched, be sure to make time for that in both your schedules. You can also spend time with your pet by teaching it to do tricks or by offering it special treats as it sits quietly on the arm of your chair as you read or watch television. Try to vary the activities when you do spend this special time with your pet so you won't fall into a rut, which can quickly become boring for both of you.

> ## I'm Bored!
> Ways of preventing boredom in your bird include rotating toys, moving your bird to a new location in the home, adding a new food item to the menu, and talking or singing to your bird.

If you notice that your bird becomes fidgety and restless during these special "together times," it may be trying to tell you that it's become bored with the situation and wants to go play on its playgym or to go have a nap in its cage. Pay attention to these signals from your pet because it may become frustrated with your inattention and may develop other unwanted behaviors, such as biting or screaming.

Preening, though not to excess, is a healthy behavior.

Behaviors That Indicate Stress

Although you may not think that your bird feels stress in your home, pet birds may truly become stressed about things. Birds are quite sensitive creatures, and they quickly react to stresses that they perceive in the home.

Let's look at a few of the things that can cause a bird to become stressed. They include a new person or pet in the home; discord between family members; loud noises; earthquakes; furniture that has been rearranged; a feeling of boredom, loneliness, insecurity, or the need to breed on the bird's part; the bird isn't receiving enough sleep; or the bird isn't eating a balanced diet. Granted, certain things such as earthquakes are outside the owner's control, but other factors in the home can be managed successfully to reduce the amount of stress all family members (birds included) feel.

Pets can show that they are stressed by something in their environment in a number of ways. They can pick their feathers; they can scream; they can bite, growl at, or hiss at their owners; they can bite their nails; or they can act like little statues, hoping no one will notice them.

It may take a little detective work on your part to determine what's causing your bird to feel stressed. Once you determine what the cause is, take the time to reassure your pet that it's really going to be okay and that all will be well. If something near the bird's cage, such as a new piece of art in the room or a new wall hanging immediately over the cage, is causing the stress, consider rearranging the room to move the stressor away from the cage, or think about removing the item from the room altogether.

If you can't determine a physical cause in your home for your bird's stress, make an appointment for your pet to be checked by your avian veterinarian. Your bird may need more sleep or a better diet in order to feel more secure in its environment.

If the stressor in your bird's life is a new pet or person, work with your bird to assure it that all is well and that you still love and appreciate it. Make special time for the bird where you only pay attention to it, and show the new pet or person how important the it is to you. With time and patience, you'll soon find that peace has been restored to your home.

Interpreting Bird Body Language

As you spend more time observing your bird, you'll learn to interpret its body language. You'll know when it's content, when it's angry, or when it needs to visit the veterinarian. Observation of your bird's behavior, posture, and physical appearance each day is an important part of your bird-owning responsibilities. Because birds are so good at hiding signs of illness, owners need to be extra observant and report any changes in their pet's appearance or behavior to your veterinarian's office promptly. If your bird is sick, a quick report of behavioral or other changes by you is the best first step on your bird's road to recovery.

Here are some examples of bird body language that bird owners need to watch out for:

Learn to recognize signs of fear and apprehension.

Aggressive birds may click their beaks in a short series of clicks, raise one foot, or lift their wings over their backs. They may also fan their tails, pin their eyes (the pupil of the eye expands, contracts, and expands again in short order) or wipe their beaks on a perch or on the cage bars. In some cases, a bird may drum its wings, lean away from its cage top, or perch with an open beak.

Defensive birds may click their beaks several times in rapid succession and raise their feet at you. They may also employ the beak-wiping technique used by aggressive birds, or they may move toward you with beak open, ready to defend their turf.

Excited birds will pin their eyes, fluff their feathers, and seem to be going countless ways all at the same time. If your bird seems like all its sensory circuits have overloaded, approach it with caution. An excited bird is likely to bite you, so leave it alone until it has had a chance to calm down.

Jealous birds may destroy their cages, bite their owners, or scream when the owner gets on the phone or tries to watch television. This problem is often easier to prevent than it is to solve, so be sure to give your bird time alone in its cage with its toys from the time you first bring it home. If your bird begins to scream, don't reward it by paying attention to it or by yelling at it. In either case, the bird gets what it wants—your attention—and this will make it only scream more the next time around. Also, take care not to bribe your pet into silence with treats when you are on the phone or when your favorite show is on because the bird will quickly learn to manipulate you into providing it with more treats.

Possessive birds may hiss or otherwise try to scare family members away from their chosen person. A possessive bird may also try to pair bond with its chosen person. It will preen that person's eyebrows, hair, fingernails, or eyelashes and will sit as close as it can to that person. It may also try to regurgitate to its chosen person. As with jealous behavior, possessiveness is often easier to prevent than to treat, so make sure all family members take care of the bird from the time it arrives in your home. Rotate feeding and cage-cleaning chores among members of the family to ensure that the bird doesn't bond more with one person than another.

Threatened birds may tap their feet in an attempt to scare away the intruder. They try to stand as tall as they can in an attempt to look large and frightening. They may also demonstrate aggressive behaviors or try to bite whatever they believe to be threatening.

Socializing Your Bird

To properly socialize your bird, you will expose it to a variety of situations and people. In all of these situations and when meeting new people, you must reassure your pet that all will be well and encourage it to explore its surroundings in order to build its confidence.

A good way to start socializing your bird is to introduce it to your house room by room during its first few days in your home. Take the bird on a tour of your place, and tell it about the different rooms in your home. Speak in a quiet, positive voice, and allow your bird to explore each room under your supervision.

When introducing new people to your bird, speak softly and enthusiastically about the person. If the person is comfortable handling birds, allow him or her to handle your bird. Otherwise, let the person pet your bird and speak to it in a quiet, reassuring way. Praise the bird for doing so well in a new situation, and reward it with a special treat, new toy, or other form of attention.

Bonding With Your Bird

The most important thing to remember as you begin to build a relationship with your bird is that you must work hard to earn your bird's trust, and then you must never do anything to betray that trust. Birds have long memories, so act in a trustworthy manner around your pet at all times. Although they don't operate in a vindictive or vengeful way, birds do remember both good and bad things that are done to them, and they are less likely to trust you completely if something bad happens to them.

Cockatoos are known for their love of snuggling.

Part 2

Behavior Problems and How To Solve Them

Sometimes, the behaviors that pets display are downright confusing to their owners. Others, such as biting, screaming, chewing, and feather picking, can harm either the owner or the bird. Although no problem behavior can be solved overnight, most can be managed effectively or prevented before they become problems.

The first thing owners need to keep in mind when trying to understand their pet's behavior is to look at the situation from the bird's point of view. What makes no sense to us when we look at the behavior with our human expectations makes better sense when we overlay some basic bird behavior on the event.

One such situation is when a bird starts to bite its owner's face while sitting on the owner's shoulder. In many cases, the owner gets his or her feelings hurt and the bird is relegated to its cage–not exactly a win-win situation. Rather than have hurt feelings, consider instead that birds often encourage their mates (which is what your bird may consider your face) to flee a dangerous situation (a flock of big, black crows that lands in a tree outside your family room window, for instance). To do so, birds will poke at or even bite their mates in order to encourage them to flee.

The best way to solve a problem such as this one is to prevent it from ever happening. Don't allow your pet bird to ride on your shoulder for starters, and pay attention to events that are occurring in your yard that your bird may find frightening. By looking at the world through your bird's eyes, you can better understand its behavior patterns and lessen the chances for behavior problems to begin.

If your bird starts to develop behavior problems, you first need to consider your behavior, because in many cases owners create situations that cause their pets to misbehave. If you like to roughhouse with your pet bird, you shouldn't be surprised if you are bitten by your pet because birds that get excited are likely to bite. If you play with your bird's beak right after mealtime, your pet will probably regurgitate its meal to you as if you were its mate or a chick in search of food. If you allow your pet to hide in the cubbyholes in your rolltop desk or if you cuddle and snuggle with it during breeding season, your bird may think you're encouraging it to breed and it may begin to display courtship and breeding behaviors of its own.

In each of these examples, the birds aren't misbehaving–they are providing normal, natural reactions and behaviors caused by actions on the parts of their owners. If anything, the owners are misbehaving by causing their pets to react in a manner that the owners find unacceptable. So before you blame your pet for what you consider bad behavior, make sure you aren't unintentionally doing something to cause the bird to misbehave. If you're the cause of the problem, take steps to alter your behavior to resolve the problem.

Parrot owners may be faced with a parrot that bites, screams, chews, or picks its feathers. Because these are some of the behaviors that cause parrot owners a great deal of concern, let's look at their causes and solutions in more detail.

Biting

First, we'll look at biting. Biting is a problem because, simply put, bird bites hurt! In most cases, the only thing injured is the owner's feelings, but bird bites can cause serious injury if the bird doing the biting is a large parrot, such as a macaw or a cockatoo.

Although bird bites sometimes seem to come out of nowhere, your bird often has what it considers a perfectly valid reason for biting. It may believe your earrings or other jewelry are acceptable chew toys, it may want you to do something that you aren't doing fast enough, or it may not want you to handle it or take it out of its cage. In all cases, your bird finds biting a normal behavior, and in all cases, you as its owner would consider biting an abnormal behavior.

In all these instances, a little behavior modification on the part of the parrot owner can help prevent a bird from biting. If you don't allow your bird to chew on your jewelry, it won't be tempted to bite you. If you don't ignore your bird's body language and other indications that it wants to go to its cage or playgym, chances are it won't bite you to hurry you along. If you pay attention to the signals your bird uses to indicate it is tired or doesn't want to interact with you at a particular time, it won't bite you to make you leave it alone.

> *Take Note*
> Although bird bites often seem to come out of nowhere, your bird often has what it considers an important and perfectly valid reason for biting.

If your bird bites you, resist the temptation to tap or grab its beak as punishment. In bird body language, you are sending the wrong message. Tapping on a bird's beak to discipline it is something that the bird won't understand, and grabbing its beak could be encouraging the bird

Biting is one habit best prevented from the start.

to fight you, to greet you, or to initiate breeding behavior—none of which are the message you're trying to send.

Because preventing a bird from biting is a much easier solution than trying to stop a well-developed biting habit, offer your parrot a wide variety of acceptable chew toys, an interesting and healthful diet, and ample opportunities to exercise outside its cage.

If your bird develops a biting habit, you may want to stop handling it because you won't be bitten if you don't handle the bird. But please continue to handle your pet because by not handling the bird, you may end up with a relationship that neither of you finds enjoyable.

Screaming

One thing parrot owners need to accept from the beginning of their relationship with a pet bird is that all birds scream at one time or another. Parrots are most likely to make noise at dawn and at sunset, and owners can often quiet their birds somewhat. However, screaming is not a behavior that you'll eliminate completely from your pet's normal routine.

The first thing to do when your bird screams is to determine the cause of the scream. Is your pet in danger? Has it gotten itself into a predicament it can't easily get out of? Does it see someone or something that it perceives as a threat? Does the bird feel that it is all alone in the house? Is it tired?

Although you cannot completely remove screaming from your bird's list of behaviors, you can take steps to minimize the screaming episodes. Give your bird a daily dose of attention, set consistent playtimes and naptimes for it, make its environment interesting, and offer your pet a varied, healthful diet to help reduce its chances of screaming.

Take Note

All parrots make noise—and even scream—at times. Understand that screaming is a behavior that you may be able to manage somewhat, but never eliminate.

If you find that your bird enjoys screaming, try teaching it to whistle or to talk rather than scream. When your bird screams, distract it by whistling or saying a word or phrase that you want the bird to learn. Praise your pet if it whistles back or repeats the word, and ignore it if replies with a scream. Your bird will likely learn this new game quickly and will want to play along because it will be rewarded with attention from you.

Chewing

Chewing is another normal parrot behavior that can be modified but not fully eliminated from a bird's routine. Parrots chew to keep their beaks in condition. Chewing can become a problem when pet parrots do not have access to a variety of acceptable items upon which they can chew, such as toys, mineral blocks, or food items. Because the bird still needs to chew, it will begin to destroy other items in the home, which are not only unacceptable but potentially dangerous. These include paneling, furniture, office supplies, electrical cords, telephones, books, antiques, appliances, and stereo equipment—in short, anything a bird can get its beak on can and will be chewed, and it usually works out that whatever you value most in your home is exactly the same item you bird selects as its newest chew toy.

Frayed and chewed feathers may indicate a health problem.

Take Note

All birds need to chew, so make it easier on both you, your pet, and your prized possessions by providing it with lots of toys and wooden objects to chew on.

Because birds need to chew, their owners need to provide an ample supply of healthy chewable items, such as toys, empty paper towel or toilet paper rolls, raw pasta pieces, or nuts in the shell. At the same time, restrict your bird's access to other items in the home that the bird might be tempted to chew on. Not only will this protect your household treasures, it will also ensure your bird's continued health and well-being.

Feather Picking

Feather picking can be caused by physical problems, emotional problems, or a combination of both. If your bird suddenly begins to pick its feathers, contact your avian veterinarian's office to schedule an appointment for an examination to rule out physical causes.

Consult an avian vet at the first signs of feather picking.

Once physical causes have been ruled out or resolved, it's time to examine the emotional issues that may cause your pet to pick its feathers. Is it getting enough sleep? Is its cage on an unsteady stand that causes the bird to feel insecure? Is another pet or person in the home causing the bird to feel stress? Does the bird have access to interesting toys? Does it have a varied routine? Was the room its cage is in recently rearranged or remodeled? Has the bird been exposed recently to a number of new people?

Look at your home environment and your bird's daily routine carefully, especially if something has recently changed in either one. If something has changed, see if changing it back will resolve the problem. If the change cannot be undone, reassure the bird that it's okay and that all will be well in its new environment.

Time and patience are required for bird owners to resolve feather picking problems in their parrots, and owners need to realize up front that some birds are never completely cured of this habit. Some birds revert to the habit in times of stress, while others have picked their feathers so completely at some point that the feather follicles themselves are damaged and incapable of producing new, healthy feathers.

Although it's difficult for us to believe, some parrots actually find the feather-picking habit soothing, which is why they keep doing it. Like some people who find solace in shopping or others who drown their sorrows in chocolate, certain parrots pick their feathers to relieve stress, boredom, or anxiety.

Problem Solving Takes Time

If your bird develops a behavior problem, realize that it will take time and patience on your part to resolve the problem. In some cases, the behavioral problem never fully resolves itself, so owners have to be careful to limit triggers that can set off episodes of problem behavior. If, for instance, your bird becomes stressed and pulls its feathers when your daughter's softball team comes over for after-game refreshments, you may have to move the bird to a quieter part of the house when the team comes over. If your bird screams every time it sees you wearing a hat, don't wear hats around your bird. If your bird likes to chew its wooden toys, don't let it near your antique jewelry box from your great-grandmother because your bird won't know the difference between that wooden box and its wooden toys.

When trying to solve your pet's behavior problems, steer clear of quick-fix solutions, such as putting the bird in a dark closet or spraying it in the face with water. These types of solutions will only damage your overall relationship with your parrot, and this could cause more problems down the road.

Take the time to evaluate what's causing your pet's behavior problem and make an effort to remove or reduce the stressors in your pet's life. Again, this will take time and require some dedication on your part, but in the end you'll have a much more well-adjusted pet, which you'll enjoy more than one that has behavior problems.

Double the Feathers, Double the Fun

You've had your first bird for a year or so, and you've decided to add another pet bird to your home. Perhaps you're thinking about setting up a pair of birds for breeding or perhaps you just want to adopt a birdie buddy for your feathered friend.

Before adopting an additional bird, make sure you have the physical space for the new bird's cage. Consider the amount of time a new bird will add to your bird-care schedule, and the amount of noise an additional bird may add to your home. Also, make sure you can afford the additional expense of food, toys, and veterinary care for an additional bird.

After you're sure you're ready to add another bird to your home, here are some tips that may make the initial introduction period easier on you and your birds:

LENA

Are you ready for an entire flock?

• Although birds are natural flock animals, it's best not to add a new bird into the same cage as your resident pet. Fights may break out between the newcomer and the resident parrot because the resident parrot will defend its territory. If you want to house birds together, introduce them to the new cage simultaneously, but don't do this until the birds are comfortable around one another. Be sure to purchase a cage that's large enough for your pets to live together harmoniously.

• Make sure you purchase healthy birds. Have any newcomers examined by your avian veterinarian and quarantine them for at least a month to prevent the potential spread of disease. During quarantine, visit the new bird's cage last, and use separate food and water bowls for it until you are sure it's completely healthy.

• After your new bird has passed quarantine, introduce your new pet and your resident pet in a neutral area away from the resident pet's cage. Set the birds' cages near each other and watch their reactions. If the birds seem interested in one another (they move toward one another, pin their eyes, fluff their feathers, or begin chattering at each other), move the cages closer to one another. If the birds don't seem interested in one another, leave the cages farther apart until you see signs of interest. Let the birds out of their cages for further interaction only after the birds seem interested in one another, and supervise the meeting to ensure the safety of both birds.

• Make sure to handle each of your pets frequently to maintain a good relationship with them. If given a choice, birds will bond with one another more strongly than they bond with humans, so you'll have to work on maintaining the relationship you have with your birds by handling them and interacting with them each day.

• Teach all your birds the "up" and "down" commands and practice them regularly. This will help you maintain control over your pets in case they begin squabbling with one another.

• Don't combine large and small birds. Large birds can easily injure their smaller companions, so try to keep the size of your pets approximately the same to ensure the health and well-being of all feathered family members.

• By the same token, consider the personalities of the species you're planning to keep together. Mixing an assertive species with a more laid-back personality may not be the ideal combination, so try to keep the temperaments of your new and your existing birds similar.

• Keep your flock's "pecking order" in mind when playing with your pet birds in order to reduce the chances of your resident pet becoming jealous of or stressed about the new bird. Some birds develop behavior problems, such as feather picking, in response to the addition of a new bird to the home.

• Supervise all interactions between your birds to reduce the chances of accident or injury.

Having more than one bird in your home doubles not only your enjoyment of your pets, but also the birds' enjoyment of each other. Many bird lovers who share their home with more than one feathered friend report that the birds learn from each other. Some learn tricks, such as opening their cage doors in tandem, while others learn words or phrases from their feathered companions. The birds will converse with one another during the day, even if their cages are kept in different rooms. In some cases, one bird in the home takes it upon itself to step in and discipline the unruly members of the flock, often correcting the misbehaving bird in its owner's voice.

Part 2

6

Feeding and Nutrition

Understanding proper parrot nutrition is a vital part of pet bird ownership. Today's pelleted bird diets have come a long way from the traditional seeds-and-water fare that was commonly offered 30 years ago when I got my first parakeet. In this chapter, we'll look at the diets that are available for pet birds, how fresh foods fit into a bird's diet, and which people foods are unhealthy for birds.

Bird Food Basics

In the wild, parrots eat a wide variety of foods. Scientists have observed birds eating seeds, fruit, nectar, pollen, berries, nuts, snails, and insects. Researchers at the Tambopata Research Center in southeastern Peru have studied the habits of macaws and other parrots that come to the center's

Wild birds spend much of their time looking for food.

Many birds, including finches, pick at food on the ground.

clay licks, and they have determined the birds eat the clay at the licks to receive minerals they cannot get in their natural diets and also to neutralize the effects of toxic foods that they consume in the jungle—a sort of parrot antacid for when they've overeaten a certain food that doesn't agree with them!

For years, we've been hearing about the basic four food groups for people—vegetables, fruits, dairy, and meat—and in recent years, the food pyramid has become popular. Although you may not believe it, the same principles of good nutrition for people can be applied to a pet parrot's diet.

Here's the diet recommended by the Association of Avian Veterinarians: 50 percent grain and legumes; 45 percent dark green or dark orange vegetables and fruits; and 5 percent meat (well cooked, please), eggs (also well cooked), or dairy products. Let's see how this applies to a possible food pyramid for a pet bird:

Starting from the pyramid's base, we first find the carbohydrate group. These would include pellets, whole grain pastas, unsweetened breakfast cereals, whole-wheat bread, cooked beans, and cooked rice.

Next would come the vegetables and fruits level. Dark green or dark orange vegetables and fruits contain vitamin A. This important vitamin, which is missing from the carbohydrates group, helps a bird fight off infections. Dark green or dark orange vegetables that are healthy for your bird include carrots, yams, sweet potatoes, broccoli, dried red peppers, dandelion greens, and spinach.

The next level of a pet parrot food pyramid would include the meats and dairy groups.

Foods in these groups that are good for your parrot include parrot-size portions of well-cooked meat, tofu, water-packed tuna, fully scrambled eggs, cottage cheese, unsweetened yogurt, or low-fat cheese. Because a bird's digestive system lacks the enzyme lactase that digests milk products, limit the amount of milk and cheese your pet receives to ensure it won't suffer digestive upsets.

The top of the food pyramid would be the pinnacle of treats. Here is where seeds, long considered the staple for parrots, should be placed. Use seeds as an occasional treat or as a reward during training sessions.

Offer your pet fresh foods such as fruits and vegetables in the morning and in the evening, and make sure it has access to pellets at all times. Remove fresh foods from the cage after about 30 minutes to keep your pet from consuming spoiled food.

Now that you know what makes up a healthy diet, let's look at foods that shouldn't be fed to your bird. These include alcohol, rhubarb, avocado (the skin and the area around the pit can be toxic); or human snack foods that are highly salted, sweetened, or fatty. Those chips, cookies, and French fries aren't good for you, and they won't do your pet's health any good, either.

For some added fun, present your bird's food in a new way.

Chocolate is particularly harmful to birds because it contains a chemical, theobromine, which birds cannot digest as completely as people can. Simply put, chocolate can kill your bird, so please don't share this treat with your pet.

Though sharing healthy people food with your bird is a good thing, sharing something you've already started to eat is a bad thing. Human saliva contains bacteria that are potentially toxic to birds, so it's best not to share partially eaten food with your bird. Share the food with your bird before you take a bite, or else get your bird its own portion or plate to ensure its health and well-being.

More About Pellets

Earlier in this section, the topic of pelleted diets came up, and you may be curious as to what a pellet is and what it's made of. Pelleted diets are made by combining a number of healthful ingredients into a mash and then making the mash into pellets of different shapes. Some pelleted diets are quite colorful and have had flavors added, while others are fairly plain.

An unlimited supply of food can lead to obesity.

A bird counts on its owner for consistent feedings.

Pelleted diets were created to offer more balanced nutrition for pet birds in a form that was easy for owners to serve to their pets. The pellets also reduce the chances for a bird to pick through its food dish in search of favorite treats and reject other, more healthful foods. Some birds accept pelleted diets quickly, while others require some persuading.

If you want to convert your pet to a pelleted diet, offer the pellets alongside or mixed in with its current diet. (Make sure your bird recognizes that pellets are food before proceeding.) Once you see that your bird is eating the pellets, increase the amount of pellets in its dish as you gradually decrease the amount of other food you serve. If your pet is hesitant to try the pellets, you may have to offer them as a garnish atop a favorite treat, such as a damp piece of broccoli or chunk of banana, to encourage your bird to try them.

Whatever method you use to convert your pet to a pelleted diet, please don't starve it into trying the pellets. Make sure you provide a variety of new foods consistently, along with familiar favorites to be sure your bird is getting enough to eat. If your pet doesn't dive right in to a new food, don't get discouraged. Remember to be patient and to praise your pet when it tries new foods.

The Organic Option

Organic foods have been commercially available to people since the 1970s. Pet bird owners who want to offer their pets organic foods have a variety of options available to them because several companies produce organic bird foods.

Organic foods are made with ingredients that are free from chemical pesticides or fertilizers. They are also made without preservatives or artificial flavors or colors. Veterinarian Greg Harrison, believes that birds should be fed organic foods because they "are extremely sensitive to the chemicals used in most contemporary farming and food processing facilities. The only way to ensure healthful, chemical-free raw ingredients is to specify that they be grown under strict organic conditions."

What's in This Stuff?

Labels on pet bird food contain a wide variety of information. Much of it can be overwhelming, especially if you're new to the world of birds. This overview of label information will help you make sense of all that fine print on the back panel of your pet's food bag or box.

According to *The Consumer's Guide to Feeding Birds*, each package of bird food must contain two labels. The label on the front is called the principal display label, and it contains the manufacturer's name, the brand of the specific food you are buying, and the quantity of ingredients contained in the food. The label on the back is the information panel, and it includes information on the food's guaranteed analysis, instructions for feeding the food, and the food's ingredients.

Spice up your African grey's life with a hot pepper.

The guaranteed analysis information gives the minimum levels of crude protein and fat, and the maximum levels of fiber and moisture. The crude protein level refers to the food's total protein content. The amount of protein that's useful to your bird depends on the food's ingredients and their quality.

Most of the commercially available bird diets have protein levels between 12.5 and 16 percent, fat levels between 4 and 6 percent, fiber levels that range between 2.5 and 11 percent, and moisture levels of about 10 percent. Because avian nutrition is a still-developing science, ask your avian veterinarian which type of diet is best suited to your bird's individual needs.

The food's ingredient list tells you about the different grains, fruits, vegetables, vitamins, minerals, and preservatives contained in the food. The manufacturer's name, address, and telephone number should also be found on the back of the label, so you have a way to get more information on your pet's food in case you have questions.

To determine which food is best for your bird, compare the labels of the brands available at your pet store. Ask your avian veterinarian for recommendations, and also ask the pet store staff. If you're adopting your bird from a private home, find out what the bird's diet consists of. Pet bird nutrition is a still-developing science, so be prepared to try different diets until you find one that's healthful and that your bird will eat.

Served Fresh Daily

Fresh foods play an important part in your pet bird's diet. In addition to providing vital nutrition, many fresh foods are also interesting to eat. Scientists have observed wild birds playing with their food, so why should pet birds be any different?

Although many fruit and vegetable seeds are bird-safe, be careful not to feed your bird apple seeds or the pits of apricots, cherries, and peaches, because they can be harmful to your pet's health.

Food and water containers should be washed and refilled daily.

There's Nothing Like Home Cooking

Some bird owners go the extra mile for their pets and offer them home-cooked meals. Some bird food manufacturers have tried to serve this part of the bird-owning market by offering a variety of soak-and-cook products featuring pasta, rice, beans, and dried vegetables and fruits. Some birds relish these treats, while others give them a more lukewarm reception. If you enjoy cooking, offer your pet a home-cooked meal from time to time to make mealtime more interesting.

Another option you can explore is baking bird bread. For this, you will need a box of cornbread mix (preferably one that requires the addition of an egg), some of your bird's favorite vegetables and some dried red peppers. Mix up the cornbread according to the package directions, and add the vegetables, dried peppers, and even the eggshells from the eggs you used to make the mix. (The eggshells provide calcium your bird needs, and they won't harm your pet.) Bake as directed and serve in small portions to your bird. Again, some birds love this treat, while others seem unimpressed by your efforts.

Food items that can double as toys:

- Corn on the cob
- Peas in the pod
- Grape halves with the seeds exposed
- Mangoes with pits
- Unsweetened cereal or raw pasta strung on a vegetable-tanned leather thong
- Papaya wedges
- Pomegranate wedges
- Nuts in the shell

Other Menu Items

Although it's not a food, water is a vital part of your bird's diet. Make sure your bird has access to clean, fresh water at all times, either in a water bowl or a water bottle. Although you may think of a water bottle as something designed for a rabbit or a hamster, many birds can and do learn to drink from a water bottle. Some catch on right away, while others are a little slower to master how the bottle works. Make sure your bird knows where the water bottle is and how to drink from it before you take the water bowl out of its dish. Water bottles are especially recommended if your bird seems to like dunking its pellets or fresh foods in its water bowl.

Resist the temptation to put vitamins or over-the-counter medications in your pet's water because such medications may actually contribute to bacterial growth in the water, and they may also make the water taste or smell funny, which may make your pet less likely to drink the water.

Another item that your bird should have in its cage is a mineral block or a cuttlebone. These items offer calcium and other essential minerals that your bird may not receive from its diet. In addition to their dietary benefits, mineral blocks and cuttlebones also offer chewing diversions.

Offer table foods, but only the healthy varieties.

Share These Foods With Your Parrot

Fresh fruits and vegetables

Well-cooked meat or eggs

Cooked or raw pasta

Unsalted nuts

Unsalted pretzels

Rice cakes

Unsweetened breakfast cereal

Low-fat cheese

Tofu

Cottage cheese

Don't Share These Foods With Your Parrot

Chocolate

Alcohol

Avocado

Rhubarb

Salty snacks, such as pretzels

Fatty snacks, such as potato chips

Greasy snacks, such as French fries

Sugary snacks, such as cookies

Fruits and veggies should form a major part of a bird's diet.

The Special Needs of Lories

Owners of lories and lorikeets will find that the diet of their pets differs from that of other parrot species. In the wild, lories and lorikeets survive on nectar, pollen, and fruits, and their tongues are specially adapted to eat this diet.

In captivity, these brush-tongued feeders require more than pellets and fresh foods in order to thrive. The specialized dietary needs of lories and lorikeets is one reason these birds are not more commonly kept as pets. Early captive lory diets were mostly liquid, and when liquid goes in an animal, the waste that's eliminated is mostly liquid, too. These liquid droppings were a major drawback to lory keeping in a pet situation.

Over time, nutritionists devised a diet that provided the nutrition lories and lorikeets need while making them more appealing as pets. The newer diets are powdered, rather than liquid, and the resulting droppings are easier for lory owners to clean up, which helps improve the birds' standing in the pet world.

Part 2

Here's To Good Health!

This chapter may be one of the most important for first-time bird owners. In it, we'll discuss the importance of routine veterinary care in maintaining your pet's health. We'll also look at some common diseases, as well as discuss some first aid measures you can take in an emergency. We'll also discuss the avian life span, the special needs of older or handicapped birds, and how to cope with the loss of a pet bird.

How To Find an Avian Veterinarian

Although we've discussed this matter in chapter 3, it's worth revisiting the topic briefly as an introduction to the veterinary care section of this book. Ideally, you'll select your veterinarian even before you bring your pet bird home. If that isn't possible, make

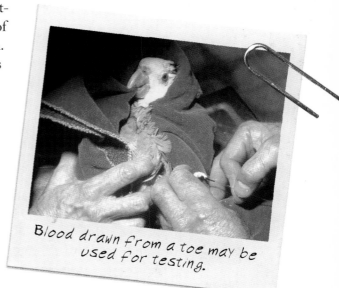

Blood drawn from a toe may be used for testing.

arrangements to find a veterinarian for your bird as soon as possible after the bird comes home for three reasons: first, you want the veterinary clinic to have some basic information about your pet when it's healthy so the staff will have a baseline to compare to in case your bird becomes ill. Second, you don't want to have to locate a veterinarian for your bird if an emergency occurs. It's far better for both your bird and you if you already know where the clinic is and what its hours of operation are before an emergency arises. Finally, most health guarantees are only valid if a veterinarian examines the bird within a specified amount of time after purchase.

When selecting a veterinarian for your bird, try to locate a doctor who is a board-certified avian specialist or a member of the Association of Avian Veterinarians. If that isn't possible, try to locate a veterinary hospital that specializes in exotic pets and that has a doctor on staff with extensive bird experience. Don't be afraid to ask the receptionist about the hospital's bird-care facilities and the experience of the staff in treating birds. Once you've selected a doctor for your bird, be sure to arrive early for your first appointment so that you can fill out all the preliminary paperwork before you actually see the doctor.

One area of avian veterinary medicine that's growing in popularity is alternative medicine. This discipline includes treatment practices such as acupuncture, herbal medicine, and Reiki. Ask your avian veterinarian for more information on alternative medical treatments that might benefit your bird.

Your First Office Visit

After you've filled out your paperwork and have been placed in an examination room, a veterinary technician will likely be the first person to examine your bird. He or she will weigh the bird, give it a visual examination and start asking you some questions about its appetite, activity level, and other indications of health. The technician's job is to help the avian veterinarian in his or her assessment of the bird. Answer all questions honestly and to the best of your ability, and ask follow-up questions of your own if you have them.

When the veterinarian comes in, he or she will take a few moments to assess your bird in its cage before taking it out to examine it. Not only does this give your bird a chance to become accustomed to the veterinarian, it also gives the doctor an opportunity to check how well your bird perches, how smooth and clean its feathers are, and how alert and active it is.

After the veterinarian has talked to you about your pet and given it a visual examination, he or she will probably take the bird out of its cage for a hands-on examination. During this examination, the veterinarian will check the bird's eyes, beak, and nostrils (or nares). He or she will feel how full the bird's chest muscles are, and he or she will gently feel the bird's legs and wings for signs of previous injuries.

In addition to the physical examination, your veterinarian may recommend laboratory tests, including blood workups or x-rays. If an infection is suspected, your veterinarian may recommend that your bird's mouth or vent be swabbed for a microbiological culture. Ask your veterinarian to explain how the tests help him or her reach a diagnosis. Also ask any questions you have about your bird's health and well-being, including questions about grooming, diet, or daily care. Your avian veterinarian and the staff of the veterinary hospital are invaluable resources because they know about the latest advances in avian nutrition and medicine.

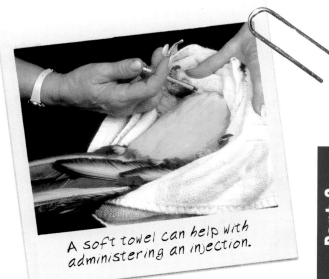

A soft towel can help with administering an injection.

Once your questions have been answered, the final step in the examination process is to discuss if any follow-up examinations are needed. If your bird is visiting the veterinary clinic for a well-bird exam, it will likely be placed on an annual examination schedule, but more frequent visits will be required if your pet is being treated for an illness or injury.

Pet Bird Health Problems

Following are some of the common medical problems that birds suffer from. Review this section carefully so you'll be able to recognize signs of illness. By knowing your bird's normal routine and acting immediately when you first notice signs that your bird is ill, you offer it the best chance of survival. Remember that birds do not often show signs of illness until they are seriously ill, so quick action is required at the first sign of sickness.

Allergies

Although avian veterinarians are unlikely to officially diagnose allergies in pet birds, a great

Signs of a Sick Bird

- bird is fluffed up all the time
- bird doesn't eat
- bird sleeps a lot
- bird's droppings look different
- bird has more (or fewer) dropping in cage
- bird's wings droop
- bird can't walk or balance on perch
- bird has food stuck on its face
- bird can't breathe easily
- bird's nose or eyes are runny
- bird is quiet all the time

Stained or fouled tail feathers may indicate illness.

deal of circumstantial evidence indicates that they do exist. Possible causes for allergies include certain foods, cage covers, pollens, molds, and dust mites. Birds that suffer from allergies will sneeze, have discharge from their noses and eyes, and they may also suffer from digestive upsets. Your veterinarian may prescribe medications for the clinical signs of allergies, and you can help improve your bird's health by limiting its exposure to substances that produce an allergic reaction, once you determine what they are.

Arthritis

Birds can develop arthritis from several different causes, such as aging, gout, or infection. Arthritic birds will have stiff, swollen joints, will become lame, and they will seem uncomfortable when trying to move the affected joint. Your veterinarian may recommend medications to relieve your pet's discomfort, or surgery may be suggested to improve the bird's condition. In addition, your veterinarian may recommend making some changes in the bird's cage, such as padded perches, to make the bird more comfortable. If the bird is overweight, it may be placed on a diet to help it feel more comfortable.

Aspergillosis

This fungal disease most commonly affects a parrot's lungs and air sacs. Parrots that have been kept in crowded, moist, poorly ventilated areas are most likely to develop aspergillosis. Parrots with this disease will breathe rapidly and wheeze. They may also have changes in their voices. Antifungal drugs are used to treat this disease, which may take months to resolve completely.

Diabetes

Like people and other mammals, birds can develop diabetes. A diabetic bird may appear excessively hungry and thirsty, and it may lose weight despite the amount of food it eats. Your veterinarian will conduct laboratory tests to determine if your bird has diabetes, and insulin injections will be prescribed once a diagnosis is made. Bird owners will have to administer regular insulin injections and will also have to monitor the bird's blood sugar level for the remainder of the bird's life.

Feather problems

Feather problems can encompass a wide variety of clinical signs, including feather picking, poor molts, or stress bars on the feathers. If you notice that your bird has begun to pick its feathers or that it doesn't molt completely, or that it's developed small holes or white lines on its feathers, contact your avian veterinarian's office for an appointment. Your veterinarian will need to examine your pet to discover the physical causes for these clinical signs.

Goiter

Goiter is an enlargement of a bird's thyroid glands that is caused by a lack of dietary iodine. Parakeets seem to be particularly prone to goiters. Birds with goiters will often have breathing problems and will attempt to swallow frequently. They may also regurgitate their food. Your avian veterinarian will provide iodine supplements that will reduce the goiter.

Gout

Birds develop gout because their kidneys are unable to fully remove the nitrogen wastes from their bodies. Birds with gout develop accumulations of uric acid either in their lower legs (in the case of articular gout) or in their internal organs (in the case of visceral gout). Your veterinarian may recommend offering more fruits and vegetables and lowering the protein level in your bird's diet. Your veterinarian may also prescribe medications that can help lower uric acid levels, as well as pain-relieving medications. Padded perches may also help make your bird more comfortable.

Physical and/or emotional issues may lead to feather picking.

Hypocalcemia

For birds, calcium is an important mineral. In addition to helping build healthy bones, it also assists with nerve transmission and muscle contraction. Some birds, such as African greys, may not receive enough calcium in their diets and may develop hypocalcemia, or low blood calcium. Affected birds develop occasional tremors or seizures. Your avian veterinarian will conduct laboratory tests to make a diagnosis of hypocalcemia, and calcium supplements will be prescribed to resolve the problem. Your veterinarian may also change your bird's diet to increase the levels of calcium it receives.

Infections

Birds can develop infections from bacterial, fungal, or viral causes. Signs of infection can include appetite loss, sneezing, nasal congestion, increased sleepiness, lack of energy, and a loss of interest in the bird's daily routine. If you notice that your bird seems sick, contact your avian veterinarian's office for an appointment. Infections do not resolve themselves on their own, and some can be difficult to resolve if they are left untreated for long periods of time.

Parasites

A variety of internal parasites can affect birds. One of the most common intestinal parasites in pet parrots is giardia, which affects primarily parakeets and cockatiels. Giardia is worth noting because it is a disease that can be passed between parrots and people. Signs of parasite infestation include loose droppings, weight loss, flaky skin, and feather picking. Your veterinarian will conduct a fecal examination to determine if your parrot has parasites, and medication will be prescribed to treat the problem.

Polyomavirus

Polyomavirus is a serious avian disease that has been known by several different names, including papovavirus and budgerigar fledgling disease. Polyomavirus is most often a disease of young birds, and it is more likely to affect a breeding aviary than a pet bird owner's home. Although the disease is most often detected by the death of a seemingly healthy young bird, other signs of polyomavirus include weakness, abdominal enlargement, bleeding underneath the skin, tremors, paralysis, or abnormal feathers. No treatment currently exists, but a vaccine is available to prevent the disease.

Proventricular dilatation syndrome

This is another serious avian disease with more than one name. It was originally called macaw wasting disease because it was first diagnosed in macaws, but it can affect many other parrot species. Although the disease is most often seen in young birds, parrots of any age may contract it. The disease affects the nerves of the digestive tract, which means that the bird cannot digest food properly. Birds with proventricular dilatation syndrome pass undigested food in their droppings, have severe weight loss, incoordination, paralysis, and general weakness. No cure exists for this disease.

Psittacine beak and feather disease syndrome

Originally known as cockatoo syndrome, the name of psittacine beak and feather disease syndrome was changed when researchers found that many parrot species can contract this disease. This highly contagious disease is most common in birds under three years of age, but birds of any age may develop the disease. Two forms—acute and chronic—of psittacine beak and feather disease syndrome occur. In the acute form, a young bird becomes depressed, develops crop problems, loses weight, and dies. In the chronic form, affected birds develop deformed feathers across their bodies, along with beak deformities and mouth ulcers. No effective treatment exists.

Psittacosis

Psittacosis is a highly contagious parrot disease that was commonly seen in imported birds (also called chlamydiosis), but is still worth mentioning today because of the limited possibility that it could be transmitted to people, especially those with compromised immune systems. Birds that have psittacosis may produce lime-green droppings, or they may show other signs of illness, such as weight and appetite loss, lack of interest in their surroundings, runny noses, and depression. People who have psittacosis show symptoms that mimic the flu, including fever, headache, runny noses, and weakness. If you have a flu bug that you just can't shake, ask your physician to test you for psittacosis. Medications are available to treat this disease in birds and in people.

Tuberculosis

This is another disease that's worth mentioning because of its potential to be passed on to humans, especially those who have compromised immune systems. Avian tuberculosis develops gradually, so signs will show themselves over time. These signs include chronic diarrhea, joint problems, or simply a bird that has been sick for a long period of time. Not all veterinarians recommend treating birds with avian tuberculosis because the disease is ultimately fatal in birds and because of the potential for this disease to be passed on to people. If your bird is diagnosed with avian tuberculosis, discuss treatment options with your avian veterinarian.

Tumors

Tumors are unusual growths that can be benign (harmless) or malignant (cancerous). They can grow almost anywhere on a parrot's body. If your bird develops a tumor, your veterinarian will conduct a biopsy to determine whether or not the tumor is malignant. If possible, he or she will also probably remove the tumor before it has a chance to grow larger.

Vitamin A deficiency

Vitamin A deficiency is a fairly common problem in pet parrots, especially those that eat a seed-heavy diet. Birds need vitamin A to keep their skin and bones healthy and to ensure they have good vision. Birds with vitamin A deficiency may have poor vision, mouth sores, frequent infections, and respiratory problems. Your avian veterinarian will conduct laboratory tests to determine if your bird has a vitamin A deficiency, and he or she will provide supplemental vitamin A. Dietary changes will also be recommended.

Parakeets are especially prone to developing tumors.

First Aid

Now that we've looked at some common pet bird medical problems, let's examine some more urgent situations that a bird and its owner might encounter. If your bird requires emergency medical treatment, be sure to contact your avian veterinarian's office immediately for instructions, and follow them even if they contradict the advice given in this book. Remember that your avian veterinarian has the advantage of knowing your bird's health history and can make the best recommendation for your pet.

Animal bites can harm your bird's health by causing the bird to go into shock from the injury itself. Animal bites can also lead to bacterial infections, which can quickly become life-threatening in a parrot, or they can cause broken bones or damage to organs and other soft tissues from the crushing action of the biting animal's mouth. The critical time period for an animal bite in a parrot is the 48 hours immediately following the bite. If your bird is bitten by an animal, have it examined by your avian veterinarian as soon as possible, even if the bird appears to be uninjured.

Beak injuries are harmful to because a bird needs its beak to be complete and functioning in order to preen and eat successfully. If you notice that your bird's beak is injured in any way, take it to your avian veterinarian for an examination.

Bleeding is a hazard because a bird's body is so small. Although birds can lose a great deal of blood without suffering long-term effects, it's best to control bleeding as soon as possible and to have your bird examined by your avian veterinarian. Bleeding can be controlled by direct pressure or by applying a cauterizing substance, such as flour or styptic powder (depending on the location of the bleeding). If bleeding does not stop shortly after the application of direct pressure or styptic powder, contact your avian veterinarian's office for further instructions.

Breathing problems are considered an avian medical emergency because breathing problems in pet birds can quickly become life-threatening situations. If your bird begins to wheeze, bob its tail, gasp for air, or make clicking noises while breathing, make sure you keep it warm and calm while contacting your avian veterinarian's office for further instructions. Putting the bird in a steamy bathroom or setting a vaporizer up near the cage may help relieve some of the breathing difficulties, but these steps cannot be considered complete solutions to the breathing problems. Rather, they are measures taken to keep the bird comfortable until it can be seen by your avian veterinarian.

A missing toe should not impede a bird's daily routine.

Broken bones can indicate serious internal injuries. Bird bones are very delicate, so the potential for fracture can be high. Fractures also require immediate

Part 2

treatment to ensure that the bird doesn't lose the ability to use a limb and to alleviate pain. If you notice that your bird has suddenly gone lame or that one wing droops lower than the other, suspect that your pet may have broken a bone and make an appointment with your avian veterinarian's office. Keep your pet warm and quiet until it is seen by your veterinarian to protect it from further injury.

Burns can be serious health threats because they can cause shock and can lead to subsequent infections. If your bird has been burned, you must first determine the cause of the burn because treatment differs depending upon the cause. Birds burned by hot water or by an alkali or acid substance should have the burned area gently flooded with cool water, while birds burned by hot grease should be treated with a light coating of cornstarch or flour. Birds that have suffered an electrical burn should have the source of the electricity turned off as soon as possible. Regardless of the cause of the burn, contact your avian veterinarian's office for further instructions about follow-up care.

Concussions can be serious threats because the bird may have sustained a severe head injury. Suspect a concussion if your bird accidentally flies into a wall or mirror, and consider concussion if the bird becomes depressed, loses its balance frequently, becomes weak, or loses consciousness. Immediate veterinary care is required to ensure your bird's health following a concussion.

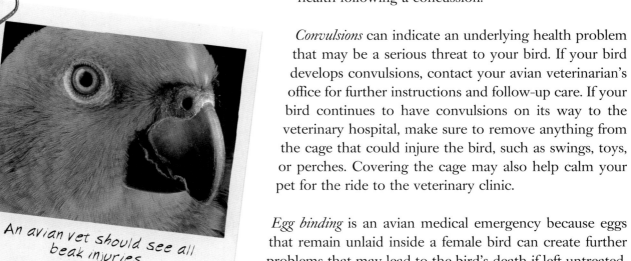

An avian vet should see all beak injuries.

Convulsions can indicate an underlying health problem that may be a serious threat to your bird. If your bird develops convulsions, contact your avian veterinarian's office for further instructions and follow-up care. If your bird continues to have convulsions on its way to the veterinary hospital, make sure to remove anything from the cage that could injure the bird, such as swings, toys, or perches. Covering the cage may also help calm your pet for the ride to the veterinary clinic.

Egg binding is an avian medical emergency because eggs that remain unlaid inside a female bird can create further problems that may lead to the bird's death if left untreated. If your female bird seems to strain to pass an egg, appears depressed and weak, or sits on the cage floor and pants, she may be egg bound. Contact your avian veterinarian's office for further instructions.

Eye injuries are considered serious medical problems because they could develop into dangerous infections or even cause a bird to become blind. If you notice that your bird suddenly has a swollen eye, blinks repeatedly, or has discharge from one or both eyes, call your avian veterinarian's office for further instructions.

Foot injuries can cause problems for a pet bird because the bird spends virtually all its life on its feet. If left untreated, foot injuries can lead to infections and other secondary health problems. If your bird suddenly becomes lame, begins favoring one foot, or develops unexplained sores or wounds on its feet, make an appointment with your avian veterinarian. Take steps to make your pet more comfortable, such as lowering perches or removing cage accessories that could become obstacles to your pet.

Frostbite is a serious medical condition in pet birds because it can result in the loss of toes or even the death of the bird. Frostbitten toes will be cold, hard, and painful to the bird. Keep the bird warm and warm the tissue slowly in a warm water bath. Contact your avian veterinarian's office for more instructions.

Heatstroke, on the other end of the temperature spectrum, is a medical emergency that can cause a bird to go into shock. Brain damage or death may result from heatstroke. A bird suffering from heatstroke will pant and hold its wings away from its body. Place the bird in front of a fan or spray it with cool water. Give the bird cool water to drink and contact your avian veterinarian's office for further instructions.

Inhaled or consumed foreign objects can obstruct a bird's respiratory or digestive system. Birds that have inhaled a seed hull or other item will show signs of respiratory distress, such as gasping or panting, while birds that have eaten a foreign object may regurgitate, have diarrhea, or pass bloody droppings. Suspect that your bird has eaten a foreign object if shows the digestive signs given above and if it was recently seen playing with a small item that suddenly cannot be found. Contact your avian veterinarian's office for further instructions.

Joint swelling can indicate a number of serious medical problems, including infection, trauma, or a joint dislocation. If your bird suddenly develops a stiff, swollen, painful joint

Part 2

or goes lame, make it comfortable and call your avian veterinarian's office for further instructions.

Lead or zinc poisoning can lead to life-threatening problems. Both create similar signs of illness, and veterinary treatment for both problems is similar. Birds with lead or zinc poisoning may be weak, lose their appetites, and show signs of neurological problems, such as convulsions, paralysis, or twitching. Other signs of lead or zinc poisoning may include regurgitation and abnormally colored droppings. Sometimes these signs appear rather quickly, while in other cases, they may develop gradually. If your bird develops these signs suddenly, contact your avian veterinarian's office for an immediate appointment. If your bird develops these signs over time, ask your avian veterinarian to test your pet for lead or zinc poisoning. Ask your avian veterinarian for more information about sources of lead and zinc in the home environment, and remove these items from your home to protect your pet from harm.

Leg bands can create problems for some birds because the bands can catch on cage bars, toys, or other items, which can cause the bird to injure itself while trying to free the caught band. Leg bands that are too tight can also cause problems because they can cut off circulation to a bird's leg. If your bird's leg suddenly looks puffy or swollen, or if the band looks tighter than normal, contact your avian veterinarian's office for an appointment. If the band catches on something in your bird's cage, do your best to calm the bird and free it, then contact your avian veterinarian's office for further instructions. The leg band may need to be removed, which is a procedure best left in the hands of an avian veterinarian.

Loss of balance may indicate a serious health problem because adult birds are notoriously sure-footed animals that rarely fall off their perches. If your bird suddenly starts losing its balance, contact your avian veterinarian's office for an appointment and take steps to protect your pet from injury, such as lowering perches in the cage or removing toys and other objects in the cage that could become obstacles for your pet.

Night frights, which are also called cockatiel thrashing syndrome or earthquake syndrome, can develop into serious situations for a pet because the bird could injure itself while thrashing. Birds that thrash will be startled while they are asleep and will try to take flight, which causes them to fly into cage bars, toys, or other objects in their cages. This can lead to damaged wing tips, feet, or chests. If your bird is prone to such episodes, put a night-light in the bird room or place your bird in a small sleeping cage without toys in it to protect it from harm.

Poisoning can cause a number of medical problems, ranging from mild stomach upset to sudden death. Suspect that your bird has come in contact with something poisonous if it suddenly starts to regurgitate, develops diarrhea, or passes bloody droppings. Poisoning should also be considered if the bird has redness or other indications of a chemical burn around its mouth, or if it suddenly becomes paralyzed. If possible, determine what poisoned your pet and put it out of reach of the bird. If your bird was poisoned by something airborne, open as many windows as you can and air out your home. Take your bird (in its cage) outdoors to get as much fresh air as possible. Call your avian

A first aid kit could save your bird's life.

veterinarian's office for further instructions and an immediate appointment.

Self-mutilation can indicate either an underlying medical or behavioral problem. Regardless of the initial cause, other medical problems can result from self-mutilation because a bird can damage its feathers, skin, or toes in the process. If you see your bird chewing or picking at its flesh, contact your avian veterinarian for an appointment.

Tissue protruding from the bird's vent is a serious medical condition. If your bird suddenly begins picking at its vent or if you notice red, brown, or black tissue sticking out of the vent, contact your avian veterinarian's office for an immediate appointment.

The Parrot Life Span

How old does an animal have to be to be considered old? Although many people don't immediately think of parrots when longevity is discussed, some pet bird species have the potential to be quite long-lived pets. Stories have circulated for years in the bird world of 100-year-old cockatoos that were often the property of some long-lost seafaring relative, but many of these stories are difficult to prove because back-up documentation is missing or the bird's history has large periods of time that cannot be accounted for. However, life

Leg bands may catch on objects or cause swelling.

spans of 50 years or more are not out of the question for some of the larger parrot species, such as macaws, cockatoos, Amazons, or African greys. With good care, some of the smaller species, such as budgerigars or cockatiels, may live 20 years or more. *The Guinness Book of Records* reported an almost 30-year-old budgerigar in Great Britain in a recent edition.

One of the more famous geriatric parrots was King Tut, a Moluccan cockatoo that served for many years as the official greeter at the San Diego Zoo. King Tut came to the zoo in 1925 and was on display near the zoo's main gate each day until 1989 (a statue on the site commemorates his service to the zoo). King Tut died a few years later after more than 60 years in captivity.

Caring for Older Birds

Avian veterinarians often think of a bird's life span in the following terms: the bird's potential life span, its expected life span, and its typical life span. Potential life spans take into account the longest-lived examples of a particular species, while the expected life span covers a time frame that is considered reasonable for that species. The typical life span is the time frame a veterinarian realistically sees in his or her practice. Unfortunately, this last category is the shortest, and birds that do not receive balanced diets and that do not live in healthy environments live short, typical lives. The good news is that birds are living longer, healthier lives, so veterinarians of the future will likely see the typical life spans of our feathered friends increase.

As pet birds become more popular pets and wild-caught pet birds become more and more a thing of the past, the care and maintenance of older pet birds will become a more important part of bird ownership.

Maximum Life Spans

African grey parrot	50 years
Amazon parrot	80 years
Bare-eyed cockatoo	40 years
Brotogeris parakeet	15 years
Budgerigar	18 years
Cockatiel	32 years
Conure	25 years
Lovebird	12 years
Macaw	50 years
Pionus parrot	15 years
Rainbow lorikeet	15 years
Rose-breasted cockatoo	20 years
Rosella	15 years
Sulphur-crested cockatoo	40 years

*Information provided by veterinarians Branson Ritchie and Greg Harrison:

Much like older people, pet birds become prone to a number of health problems as they age. These can include tumors, vision problems, thyroid gland insufficiencies, chlamydiosis, upper respiratory infections, gout, and arthritis. Though it's difficult to determine the age of wild-caught pet birds with any degree of accuracy, domestically raised birds will have their hatch dates recorded by their breeders. Some indications of old age in pet birds include a gradual lessening of the bird's activity level, poor feather condition, drooping eyelids, and facial wrinkles.

Some species, such as parakeets, can develop tumors as early as age five, although if a bird passes the age of seven without developing a tumor, it probably won't develop a tumor in its lifetime. If you notice that your pet's breastbone sticks out a little more than it used to or that your bird has difficulty perching, schedule an evaluation with your avian veterinarian because both of these signs indicate possible tumor development. Tumors develop in pet birds most frequently in the nerves off the bird's spine. A tumor in this spot can cause problems with the proper functioning of a bird's kidneys or its reproductive organs, and it can also put pressure on the nerve that runs into the bird's leg.

An African grey's neck is immobilized with a collar.

Vision problems can show themselves in several ways. Your pet may no longer be able to judge distances well, or its eyes may appear clouded over. Older birds can develop cataracts, which can be removed in some cases.

Thyroid problems occur frequently in older birds, but they aren't discussed often. These problems occur in two main areas: a deficiency in the bird's hormonal system or a need for supplemental iodine in the diet. If your parrot suddenly gains weight and develops fat deposits that resemble tumors, contact your avian veterinarian to have your pet examined.

Although they may not seem to be connected, a thyroid problem may show itself in a longer-than-average molt. If you notice that your pet seems to molt for longer and longer periods as it gets older, discuss the situation with your avian veterinarian. He or she may want to prescibe a hormonal supplement to help keep your bird healthy.

Although it's not particularly a disease of old age, chlamydiosis (also known as psittacosis) is worth mentioning. Some birds carry this disease all their lives, but they may not show signs of being infected until late in life. These signs can include diarrhea and nasal discharge. Although it doesn't happen often to pet owners, chlamydiosis can be transmitted to people, too, so alert your physician if you have flulike symptoms, including fever and an upper respiratory infection that doesn't go away. Antibiotic treatments are required for both birds and people to cure chlamydiosis.

Some older birds develop articular gout, which is a degenerative disease that affects a bird's feet and legs. Signs include swollen joints that are warm to the touch, lameness, and deposits of urate crystals under the skin of the bird's feet and legs. These masses may have to be removed surgically in order to make the bird more comfortable. Birds with articular gout may also have kidney problems.

Arthritis is another disease of old age that's sometimes seen. Birds with old injuries or those with underlying infections or metabolic problems may be more prone to arthritis. Signs of arthritis include swollen joints and a loss of use of the joint.

Owners of older pet birds may need to make some adjustments in their care routine as their pets age. If your bird has arthritis or gout, for instance, padded perches may help make it more comfortable. The cage perches may need to be lowered if your bird has trouble holding onto its perch, or they may need to be replaced with platforms to help your bird feel more secure and comfortable. If your bird has trouble climbing the cage bars, it may need bars that are more closely spaced together.

If your bird's eyesight is beginning to deteriorate, it's important to keep its food and water bowls in the same place and make sure the bird knows where they are so it can continue to eat and drink properly. Many birds that have lost much of their eyesight are still able to find their food and water bowls, and they navigate around their cages with confidence as long as their owners don't rearrange the placement of the cage accessories.

Although older birds are far from being delicate "hothouse flowers," owners of these birds should pay more attention to their pets' diets to ensure that the bird continues to receive a varied diet that is low in fat. It is also important to monitor the temperature of the room in which the bird is kept during cool weather. Add supplemental heat by using an incandescent bulb covered with a reflector on one end of your bird's cage. This allows a bird to move closer to the heat source if it is cold and away from it if the bird becomes too warm. Make sure that the bulb is far enough away from the cage so that your pet cannot burn itself on the reflector or the bulb.

One thing owners of older birds need to be on the lookout for is a change in feather color. Unlike we humans, birds do not "go gray" as they age, so any change in feather color should be noted and reported to your avian veterinarian. Causes of feather color change include protein deficiency, vitamin imbalance, or other underlying diseases that require veterinary care to treat properly.

Birds With Special Needs

In certain cases, birds that have physical handicaps or long-standing medical conditions are offered for adoption. Although your heart may go out to such animals, think long and hard about what adopting a bird with special needs may mean. Sometimes it's as simple as modifying a cage to accommodate a bird with a leg problem, but in other cases, the bird may require a regimen of medications that have to be given at certain times every day. What may seem like a minor inconvenience may become a major annoyance over time.

An avian vet may suggest mineral blocks or other supplements.

I used to bird-sit a parakeet that had a variety of physical problems. He was given to a friend of mine by a breeder. The bird had been injured in the nest by its mother and had a splayed leg and a drooping wing. The breeder knew the bird could not be sold, but she did not have the heart to destroy him because he had a charming personality. In the right home, she knew he would thrive.

To meet the bird's physical needs, my friend searched high and low for a suitable cage for her pet. She finally found one in the small animal section of her local pet store. It was designed to house a hamster and had ramps and platforms on which the hamster could climb and rest. It was perfect for her parakeet, and he settled right in to his new home.

My own parrot had a variety of physical and emotional problems. When I first adopted her, she was feather picked from below her beak to her vent and across the tips of both wings. She had tapeworms and seizures. She shook frequently, which made her veterinarian think she had epilepsy or another neurological problem. She growled and tried to bite me whenever I came near her cage. She had been advertised as a talking, singing, and whistling bird, but I saw little signs of those qualities during the first few weeks.

Over the course of the ten years I owned her, my "free" bird cost me many hours of caretaking time and thousands of dollars. Subsequent tests showed that she did not have epilepsy, but she was brain damaged, either from the capture process in Africa or from falls in her previous home. She had frequent bouts of bacterial, fungal, or viral infections that required regular doses of medication and veterinary visits.

Her veterinarian first insisted that her diet (sunflower seeds and water) be improved. So I spent a great deal of time in the produce department of my local market, trying to find healthful vegetables and fruits for her. I also tried a variety of different formulated diets before finding one that she would eat and that her veterinarian approved of.

She couldn't, or didn't, walk much. This meant she needed a special cage with a floor that had tight wire mesh so she could move around by putting one foot down, then balancing with her beak and the first foot while she adjusted her other foot into position. She continued to shake, especially when presented with a new situation or new people to meet. As her comfort level increased in a new situation, the shaking would subside, but it never completely went out of her behavior routine. She didn't talk at all the last eight years I owned her. She never sang and she rarely whistled.

What she did do, though, was worm her way into my heart. She became my best friend and almost constant companion. Most of her feathers grew back and a sweet personality emerged from behind those growls and attempts at biting. When her health failed and she had to be euthanized, I was devastated. It was more than a year before I even thought about adopting another bird.

Other bird owners share their lives with very special birds. These birds have some sort of physical impairment that makes them less than perfect to look at, but no less perfect a companion. Read on to learn what the owners of these birds did to improve the quality of their pets' lives:

Take the case of Cuddles, a cockatiel with a leg injury that makes it difficult for her to perch normally. To help her live as full a life as possible, his owner has modified Cuddles' playgym to meet her needs. Cuddles has an additional perch attached to the side of her gym that serves as a grab bar for her bad foot. She scoots around her gym, using the grab bar as she needs to and seems to have a happy, full life, according to her owner.

Beaker the cherry-headed conure is another bird with special needs. Beaker's owners found him on the cage bottom one morning, paralyzed and barely breathing. They rushed him to the vet's office, where he was treated for a possible spinal injury. Beaker's recovery process left him unable to perch for several months, so his owner replaced the perches in his cage with horizontal ladders to make it easier for the bird to get around his cage. Ladders were also added to give Beaker easier access to his new structures.

An African grey named Quasimoto suffered from curvature of the spine as a chick. His owners tried traction, physical therapy, and other treatments to give their pet as much mobility as possible. By the time the bird was eight weeks old, he was able to stand unassisted. His owners report that he doesn't walk as easily as a normal bird would, but otherwise he appears normal. However, he was unwilling to be near people, perhaps because of memories of the traction and physical therapy treatments he underwent early in life. His owners patiently worked with him to condition him to enjoy being around people again. In time, Quasimoto learned to accept kisses or head scratches as his owners passed his cage.

When A Bird Dies

For bird owners, many times the death of a pet is completely unexpected because birds are so good at hiding signs of illness. The bird seems fine at bedtime, but the owner finds it dead on the cage floor the next morning. The loss seems doubly hard to bear because it came as such a complete surprise and catches the owner completely unprepared.

Even when you have a chance to prepare yourself, the death of a pet bird is unbelievably

Nail chewing may signal nervousness.

painful. Although I knew my parrot's health was failing for several months before she was euthanized, the news that she had suffered a dramatic weight loss and developed a heart murmur caught me completely off guard. Because her quality of life was deteriorating, I believed it was time to let her go. I made this decision after discussing the situation with her avian veterinarian, who had been treating her for the past five years. We thought it best to let this special little bird go rather than have her suffer needlessly in order to keep her alive for a few more months. However, that decision hurt both of us deeply, and it also caused a number of other staff members at the veterinary hospital to mourn her passing.

Helping Children Cope

Children may have more difficulty facing the loss of a pet bird than adults in your home. The following are some suggestions to help your child cope.

Tell your child that the bird died. Although some parents might think they are "sparing" their child's feelings by not telling the child that his or her pet had died, they aren't. Invariably, the truth always comes out, and if your child finds out about the bird's death from another source, he or she not only has to deal with the death of the bird but also having his or her trust in you betrayed because you told a lie. You don't have to go into detailed explanations about the death, but you should be honest and explain as much as you can. Ask your veterinarian if he or she will speak with your child further about the bird.

Keep these pointers in mind when discussing the death of your pet bird with your child:

Do offer clear, understandable, sympathetic explanations.

Don't offer explanations that may do more harm than good, such as "The bird didn't like it here with us and it flew away." or "The bird went to sleep."

Do let your child know that feeling sad and grieving for the bird are normal, perfectly acceptable reactions to the situation.

Do allow your child to share and express his or her feelings openly.

Don't tell your child "Big kids don't cry." or "It's just a bird."

Do pay attention to your own feelings of loss and grief.

Do provide a positive role model during the grieving process.

Do communicate with your child that you understand how he or she feels and encourage him or her to continue discussing his or her feelings as long as is necessary.

Tell your child it's okay to be sad about the bird's death. Go through photo albums that have photos of the bird and child together, talk about good times the child enjoyed with the bird or about special tricks the bird did. Have your child write a letter to the bird or write a story or poem about the bird or about how he or she feels now. Let the child know his or her sad feelings will pass with time.

Don't minimize the loss by saying "It was only a bird" or "We'll get another one soon" because comments such as these may make you seem insensitive in your child's eyes. Such comments may also cause your child to become frustrated and angry with you because you don't appear to understand the depth of his or her loss.

Signs of Grief in Children

Crying

Bewilderment

Anger

Guilt

Depression

Fear of abandonment

Nightmares

Loss of sleep

Loss of concentration

Your child's reaction to the bird's death will depend on his or her age. Children under the age of five often do not understand the finality of death. They may think that something they did or thought caused the bird to not come back, or they may expect the bird to return like a perennial flower does. Explain the circumstances of the bird's death as simply and clearly as you can, and gently emphasize that the bird won't be coming back.

Part 2

Older children (those between the ages of 5 and 12) may want to know all the details of the bird's death. For this age group, honest answers seem to be the best way to help them cope with the loss. Let your child's teacher know about the bird's death, too, so that he or she can be sensitive to changes in your child's school routine that might be part of the grieving process.

Teenage children may have the hardest time dealing with the bird's death because it may seem childish for them to express emotion over the loss of the bird, yet they may be feeling the loss deeply. Encourage teenage children to express their emotions–either verbally, through artwork such as drawings or photo collages, or through writing. Let them know that adults express emotions over the loss of a beloved pet, and that it isn't strange or weird to feel sad because the bird died.

In time, begin discussing the possibility of a new pet with your child. Explain that the new bird won't replace the one that died, but it will give your family a chance to continue to experience the joys of pet bird ownership. If your child seems anxious to rush out and replace your bird immediately, encourage him or her to wait at least a few weeks before bringing home a new bird. If your child is reluctant to become attached to another bird right away, wait a few weeks and bring up the subject again. Don't push or pressure your child into bird ownership, but keep the communication lines open so that your child can let you know when he or she is ready for a new pet.

Losing a bird can be traumatic, so take time to grieve.

While helping their children cope with the death of a pet, parents need to remember that it's okay for adults to feel sad, too. Keep in mind the following quote from veterinarian William Kay, former chief of staff of the Animal Medical Center in New York City: "Grief over the loss of a pet simply denotes love for a pet. And it really is okay to love a pet completely. The love is more than returned." Don't diminish your feelings of loss by saying "It's only a bird." Pets fill important roles in our lives and our families. Whenever we lose someone close to us, we grieve.

The timetable for adding a new pet bird to your home is up to you. Some people feel the pain of loss so deeply that they are reluctant to bring home a new bird, while others adopt a new bird in short order after a bird's death. Discuss your situation with your bird's veterinarian to make sure you aren't exposing your new bird to possible harm from a contagious disease before bringing home your new feathered friend.

In my case, I didn't adopt a bird until more than a year after my bird's death. I wanted a chance to not only mourn my loss but also to celebrate my bird's life and her special place in mine. In addition to losing her, my life underwent a number of other significant changes in the year following her death. I bought a home, moved, and redecorated. Now that I'm settled in my new home and my new life, it's time to find another special bird to bring home.

When A Bird is Left Behind

Sometimes, the bird-owner relationship ends when the owner dies. Many bird owners I know have already made arrangements for their birds to be cared for after the owners die. In some cases, bird owners make care provisions for their birds in their wills. In other situations, the owners have discussed the care of their pets with trusted family members or friends who will take the bird after the owner dies.

If you are planning to address the care of your pet bird in your will, you need to know that birds are legally considered property. This means you can't make your pet bird your worldly goods. You also cannot make a pet bird the direct beneficiary of a trust. But you can plan for your bird's care after your death, and your will is a good place to do this.

To arrange for your pet bird's care in your will, legal experts recommend that you establish a trust in which you leave the bird (along with money to be used for its care) to a friend or relative who is named as beneficiary of the trust. Be sure to talk about your plans with the person you want to care for your bird so that person and your bird have a chance to interact and get to know one another well in advance of the trust being put into place. State laws about wills and trusts differ, so make sure to discuss your situation with your lawyer, too.

If you have no bird-loving friends or family members, you may want to investigate the possibility of placing your pet in a bird refuge or sanctuary. Ask your avian veterinarian for more information on these "bird retirement centers."

Now let's look at the situation from a different point of view: you've just inherited your favorite aunt's parrot, which she owned for 40 years. When you take over the care of this bird, keep in mind that it misses your aunt greatly and will need to grieve that loss. The bird may eat poorly, seem depressed or begin to pick its feathers. Try to be as patient and understanding as you can during this time. Remember that the bird has lost someone it cared about a lot, too. Also, its normal routine is gone, and settling into your home will take time.

Looking Good

Grooming your parrot is an important part of bird ownership. Birds need to have clean, well-maintained feathers to look and feel their best. Regular bathing encourages birds to preen their feathers, which helps the feathers stay in top condition.

In addition to bathing, birds need to have their wings and nails trimmed regularly to ensure their well-being and safety. Clipped wings lessen the chance of a bird escaping from your home and flying away, while trimmed nails are less likely to cause harm to a bird because they cannot get caught on a toy or in your carpet as quickly as untrimmed nails can.

One aspect of grooming that your pet bird probably

Learn grooming skills from someone with experience.

Part 2

won't need your help with is keeping its beak trimmed. Healthy pet birds with an adequate supply of chew toys should be able to keep their beaks in condition. If you notice that your bird's beak is overgrown, take it to your veterinarian's office for a beak trim and an examination because excessive beak growth can indicate an underlying medical problem. Don't try to trim your pet's beak by yourself because the beak contains a number of blood vessels, which is why trimming is best left to your avian veterinarian.

Don't Do It
Never attempt to trim your bird's beak by yourself. An avian veterinarian should examine and treat any excessive or abnormal growth.

Bathing

Pet birds can bathe in several different ways. Some smaller birds, such as parakeets or cockatiels, like to use special birdie bathtubs that fit inside the cage, while others find rolling in damp greens refreshing. Still other birds enjoy being misted with warm water, while others like to stand in the sink and take a shower under a gentle stream of water. Some larger species even enjoy showering with their owners, and special shower perches that attach to the side of the shower stall with suction cups are available.

Find out which bathing method suits your pet bird best and be sure to allow it the chance to bathe regularly. Make sure your bird bathes early in the day so that its feathers have an opportunity to dry before bedtime. Some birds would bathe every day if they had the chance, but others are content with a bath every few days or every week. Determine a schedule that suits your bird's needs and stick to it.

Although you might be tempted to add soap or special feather-conditioning agents to your bird's bath, you won't need to provide your pet with anything more than clean water in most cases. Detergents can remove the protective oils from a bird's feathers, and feather conditioners may actually cause a pet bird to start picking its feathers in an attempt to clean them and remove the conditioners.

Shower perches are great for birds that love a good spray.

Nail Trimming

Nail trimming can be a simple procedure if you're fortunate enough to own a bird with light-colored nails. Light-colored nails let you see where the nail stops and the quick (the nail's nerve and blood supply) begins. Bird owners need only trim off the nail's hooked portion to protect their pets from injuring themselves by catching a nail on their cages or toys. If your bird has dark-colored nails, you may want to have your avian veterinarian's office trim your pet's nails to ensure the nails aren't cut too deeply.

Nail-Trimming Supplies

To trim your pet's nails safely, you will need to have the following items available:

√ An assistant who will hold the bird as you trim the nails

√ A towel in which to wrap your pet during the nail-trimming process

√ Nail clippers of an appropriate size for your bird (human nail clippers work well for small birds, while dog nail clippers are recommended for larger birds)

√ Styptic powder to control bleeding if you cut a nail too deeply

√ A nail file to smooth off the rough edges as you trim

Start by having your assistant catch your bird in a towel (see the "Going Home" chapter for information on how to handle and towel a bird). Be sure to allow your bird's chest to rise and fall naturally during the toweling process to ensure that its breathing is not restricted.

Uncover one foot and begin trimming the nails. Trim off only a small amount of the hooked part of the nail. File the cut nail to protect your pet from catching a rough nail edge on a toy or on the carpet of your home.

Uncover the other foot and trim nails. File nails after trimming.

Use a nail file to smooth out rough edges after clipping.

Release bird from towel and reward with treats or extra attention.

Some bird owners find it easier on both them and their birds to have the bird's nails trimmed at the veterinarian's office or at a bird specialty store by a bird groomer. If you find you or your pet are extremely stressed out by a pedicure, investigate other grooming options.

Wing Trimming

Wing trimming is a slightly more complicated process than nail trimming. A proper wing trim should prevent a pet from flying away while still giving the bird enough wing feathers to glide safely to the ground if it is startled while atop its cage. Wing trimming must be done carefully because it's very easy to injure a bird while trimming its wings. Most bird owners don't towel and restrain their birds often enough to keep their restraint skills sharp. For this reason, it's best to have your avian veterinarian's office trim your pet's wings.

Don't Do It
Canaries and finches usually do not need to have their wings clipped.

If you are unable to have your veterinarian trim your bird's wings, here's what you will need to complete the task, along with step-by-step instructions to complete the process.

Wing-Clipping Supplies

√ an assistant to hold the bird safely as you clip the wings

√ a well-worn towel (appropriate to the size of your bird) to wrap your bird in

√ small, sharp scissors

√ needle-nosed pliers in case a blood feather is cut and must be removed

√ styptic powder to stop bleeding (direct pressure on the site of bleeding also works well)

Set up your supplies in a well-lit area, such as on your dining room table. You'll need a spot that's large enough to lay your bird out on its back and spread its wings. Have your assistant safely towel your bird and remove it from its cage.

Lay the bird on its back and spread out one wing. Before you begin cutting, check blood feathers. Blood feathers are those feathers that are still growing in, and you can easily see them on your bird's wing. Their tight appearance and quill-like look give them away. Delay wing clipping if your bird has a lot of blood feathers growing in. These feathers need a chance to develop further before trimming.

To clip your bird's wings, start at the wing tip and work inward. Carefully cut each fully developed flight feather.

Part 2

Trim the feathers to the line formed by the ends of the feathers above the flight feathers on the wing. Cut the first six to eight feathers on each wing.

The number of feathers you cut will depend on the size and shape of your bird's body. Remember that the longer and leaner the body type, the more feathers you'll have to trim. African greys have short, chunky bodies and need to have fewer feathers trimmed than cockatiels, which have long, slender bodies.

Repeat the wing-trimming process regularly to ensure your bird's safety. Check the length of the flight feathers each month, and trim the feathers when they've grown out enough for your bird to start trying to fly. Most birds have their wings trimmed about every three months, but you will have to set up a schedule that meets your bird's needs.

Now, let's talk a little more about the blood feathers I mentioned earlier. In the course of wing trimming, even the most careful groomer will occasionally cut or break a blood feather. If this happens to you, first remain calm. Then the bleeding must be stopped and the feather removed. To stop the bleeding, pack the feather with styptic powder and take the bird to your veterinarian's office or an animal emergency clinic. Call ahead to make sure someone will be available to treat your bird promptly upon your arrival at the vet's office or clinic.

Some owners prefer to let a vet perform required wing trims.

If you prefer to remove the feather yourself, your assistant will need to hold the bird's wing steady. You will grasp the broken feather's shaft as close to the skin of your bird's wing as you can with needle-nosed pliers. As you pull the feather out completely, your assistant will apply equal and opposite pressure from the other side of the wing. Once the feather is out, put direct pressure and a pinch of styptic powder on the spot you removed the feather from until the bleeding stops. If the bird continues to bleed after you've applied direct pressure for a few minutes or if you aren't able to remove the feather shaft, call your avian veterinarian's office for more instructions.

While you may think you're hurting your bird as you pull out the broken blood feather, realize that a broken blood feather could bleed a lot, and the longer the feather stays in, the more the bird bleeds. Once the feather shaft is pulled out, the bird's skin generally pulls together and stops the flow of blood.

Feathers

What one thing sets birds apart from all other animals? Why, it's their colorful feathers, of course. Those feathers and the fact that they enable birds to fly help make birds unique in the animal kingdom.

Whether it's your pet parrot in a cage in your living room or wild birds at a feeder in your backyard, you can see a veritable rainbow of colors in bird feathers. They range from the snow white of cockatoos and doves; to the pink of a Major Mitchell's cockatoo; through the brilliant red of cardinals, macaws, and lories; from the rich orange of a Baltimore oriole or a sun conure, to the brilliant yellow of a golden conure or a goldfinch; through the vibrant green of the Amazons; to the festive blue of the blue jay; through the majestic purple of a hyacinth macaw or purple martin to the glossy black of the crow.

Why do birds even have feathers? Well, birds need feathers to help them fly, to keep them warm, to attract mates, to help line their nests and to frighten predators. Feathers are lightweight, complex, extremely strong structures that are thought to have evolved from the scales of reptiles, but scientists are still searching for the stages of development between scales and feathers.

The number of feathers a bird has on its body varies greatly from species to species. For instance, a parakeet has between 2,000 and 3,000 feathers on its body, while a cockatiel has between 5,000 and 6,000 feathers on its body. In the wild, feather counts range from about 1,000 for a ruby-throated hummingbird to more than 30,000 for an emperor penguin.

Regardless of species, a bird's feathers grow from follicles that are arranged in rows that are known as pterylae. The unfeathered patches of bare bird skin between the feathers are called apteria.

A feather can be broken down into its component parts from base to tip. The calamus is the stubby, tubelike end of a fully developed feather that is found beneath a bird's skin. This end is also sometimes called the quill or base of the feather shaft. The calamus is hollow and light, but surprisingly strong. Rising from the calamus or quill is the rachis, which is the long portion of the feather shaft that is seen above the skin surface. From it branch the barbs and barbules (smaller barbs) that make up what we normally think of as the feather. These structures have small hooks on them that allow the feather parts to join together to create the feather's vane.

Another important, but sometimes overlooked, part of a bird's feather is the pulp, which is found in the center of a growing feather. Feather pulp provides a blood supply to the growing feather, and it gradually decreases as a feather grows. Feather pulp is important because it is what is analyzed during a feather sexing procedure to determine a bird's gender.

Birds have several different types of feathers on their bodies. These include the contour feathers, coverts, remiges, rectrices, down feathers, powder down feathers, semiplumes, filoplumes, and bristles. Each fulfills a particular function for the bird. They are as follows:

Contour feathers are the largest and most colorful feathers, which are seen on a bird's body and wings. They cover the bird and give contour to its body, which is how they got their name.

When necessary, a feather should quickly be pulled from its base.

Coverts are specialized contour feathers that are found on a bird's wings and tail. These feathers overlap the larger flight feathers on a bird's wing and complete the flight surface. Five sets of coverts may be found on a parrot's wing.

Remiges are the flight feathers found on a bird's wing. They are further divided into primary and secondary flight feathers. The primary flight feathers are found between the bird's elbow and its digits, while the secondary flight feathers are located between the bird's body and its elbow.

Rectrices are the tail flight feathers.

Down feathers are frequently seen on young birds. As the birds develop, their down feathers are replaced with more mature plumage. However, down feathers exist on adult parrots, too. They help keep a bird warm.

Powder down feathers are found on only a few parrot species. African greys, cockatiels, and cockatoos have powder down feathers, which create a powdery substance as the birds preen them. This substance helps the birds keep their feathers in condition, but it also may cause allergies in susceptible owners.

Semiplumes help keep a bird warm. They are so named because of their long shafts and fluffy vanes.

Filoplumes are hairlike feathers that have long shafts and fluffy tips. They help a bird monitor and adjust the position of other nearby feathers.

When Feather Colors Mean Trouble

Pay attention to any color changes you may notice in your bird's feathers. These may be most noticeable after a molt. Some color changes are normal, such as when a bird molts into its adult plumage, but others may indicate a nutritional deficiency, the over- or under-use of vitamins, or an underlying health problem. If your bird's feathers are a significantly different color after a molt, contact your avian veterinarian's office for more information.

Bristles are specialized feathers that help a bird sense things about its environment. They are most often seen around a bird's eyes, mouth, or nares.

Feather Colors

Now that we've looked at the structure of feathers, let's look next at their color. Just exactly how do feathers take on the different colors? According to veterinarians Walter Rosskopf and Richard Woerpel, bird feather color results from pigments within the feather or from structural colors, which are cell or oil layers within the feather tissue that diffract light and create iridescent shades. Pigments within the feather can include carotenoids or lipochromes, which create red, orange, or yellow, and melanins, which create black, gray, or brown.

Sometimes, a bird's diet can influence the color of its feathers. Think of flamingoes you may have seen at the zoo.

Were they a vibrant "flamingo pink" or were their feathers more of a pastel hue? Flamingo feather color is heavily influenced by the amount of carotenoids the bird consumes each day. The same holds true in the pet bird world. Red factor canaries and some finches need color supplements in their diets to maintain the vibrant colors of their feathers, but most parrot species do not require any special supplements to maintain their feather colors.

Breeders can also use genetics to influence a bird's feather color. Over time, breeders can selectively breed to produce a particular color, or a new color may spring up without warning in a breeder's aviary. In either case, this color change is called a mutation, also described as a change in the bird's original coloring. Some species of parrot have been kept in captivity long enough that breeders have been able to develop a number of color mutations. This situation is most often seen in parakeets and cockatiels, but it also occurs in lovebirds, Quaker parrots, *Psittacula* parakeets, and grass parakeets.

Despite what you may think, mutations are not always created in horror movies following catastrophic events. In its simplest terms, a mutation is a change. When speaking of pet birds, mutations refer to dramatic or subtle changes in color or wing marking captive birds have gone through over the years. Parakeet experts estimate that about 1,800 mutations are possible. Parakeets are the most popular pet bird species and they have been bred in captivity longer than any other species of pet bird, so we'll focus on their colors as examples of mutations.

Before we proceed further, a brief discussion of some parakeet genetics terms may be in order.

What Are Those White Lines?

Birds sometimes develop what's called stress bars on their feathers. These show up as either white lines or small holes on a feather. They form when a developing feather is damaged. A bird that becomes ill or overly stressed during feather growth may also be prone to developing stress bars on its feathers. If you notice white bars across your bird's feathers, make an appointment with your avian veterinarian's office for an evaluation.

Part 2

A bird with stress bars should be examined by an avian vet.

Parakeets have 16 pair of chromosomes (people have 32), and these chromosomes determine the parakeet's color and gender. The bird's genetic makeup (or genotype) also determines its physical appearance (or phenotype). Birds can have similar outward appearances, yet have different genetic backgrounds. Chromosomes are further subdivided into sex chromosomes (parakeets inherit one pair of these) and autosomes (the chromosomes that determine all the bird's other characteristics).

Genes are either dominant or recessive. As the name indicates, dominant genes dominate recessive ones, unless a bird inherits the same recessive gene from each of its parents. Then, the recessive characteristic (such as coloration or wing markings) shows itself in the bird's appearance. This same bird would be considered homozygous for the recessive trait, while another bird that had inherited both recessive and dominant genes for this trait from its parents would be called heterozygous for the trait. Heterozygous birds are sometimes described as "splits" because pairing them with the right mate can bring out the hidden split trait.

The last bit of parakeet genetic information you need to know before we start our discussion of color mutations is that sex chromosomes in male parakeets are referred to as ZZ and females are ZY, which differs from the XY used to designate human male chromosomes and XX for human females.

In the wild, parakeets were originally green. Yellow was the first mutation reported in the wild, and it was created in captivity in the early 1870s. The blue mutation developed about ten years later, followed closely by skyblue in 1882. These mutations were followed by dark green in 1915, olive green in 1916, white and cobalt in 1920, gray wings in the early 1920s, mauves in 1924, the crested topknot mutation in the 1920s in Australia, and violets in the late 1920s. Lutinos followed in the 1930s; albinos and cinnamons in 1931; Danish recessive pieds and fallows in 1932; clearwings, grays, and opalines in 1933; and yellowfaces and dominant pieds in 1935.

The Second World War hampered parakeet color development (among other things). Parakeet breeding picked up again in the 1950s, and more mutations developed, including lacewings, dark-eyed clears, and spangles.

Some parakeet characteristics—pied, clearwing, graywing, dark-eyed clear, fallow, blue, and dilute—are considered recessive characteristics. To create these colors, both parents must carry a recessive gene.

Some other parakeet characteristics—cinnamon, albino, lutino, opaline, and red-eyed lacewings—are termed sex-linked traits, which means they can be inherited from one or both parents.

Mutations can be simply divided into two groups: colors and wing marking and patterning. The colors are green, gray, blue, violet, lutino, albino, white, yellow, dark-eyed clears, pied (dominant), and pied (recessive). The wing marking and patterning mutations are cinnamon, pied (clear-flighted), graywing, whitewing, yellow wing, lacewing, opaline, fallow, and spangle. Other varieties, such as cresteds and "dusters," will be discussed later.

Light Green is the normal color of wild parakeets. These birds have buttercup yellow masks with three clearly defined black spots on each side of the throat and violet cheek patches. Their general body color is a solid, bright grass-green, with black, well-defined markings on cheeks, back of head, neck, and wings. Their long tail feathers are blue-black. *Dark Green* birds have dark laurel-green body color and darker tail feathers. *Olive Green* birds have deep olive-green bodies and tail feathers that are darker in proportion.

Light Yellow birds have buttercup-colored faces, backs, rumps, breasts, flanks, wings, and underparts. Their primary flight feathers are lighter than their body feathers, and their long tail feathers are lighter than their body color. *Dark Yellow* birds resemble their light yellow counterparts, but the dark birds have deeper color on their body feathers. *Olive Yellow* resemble light yellow birds, too, but olive yellows have mustard-colored body feathers.

Skyblue parakeets have clear white face masks that are ornamented on each side of throat with three clearly defined black spots, one of which appears

Birds may experience some discomfort while new feathers are emerging.

Part 2

at the base of the cheek patch. Their cheek patches are violet, and their bodies are pure skyblue. Markings on the cheeks, back of head, neck, and wing of a skyblue parakeet are black and well-defined on a white ground. These birds have long, blue-black tail feathers.

Cobalts resemble their skyblue relative, but their bodies are a rich deep cobalt blue. with their long tail feathers darker in proportion. *Mauves* are similarly colored, but they have purplish mauve body feathers, with a tendency toward a pinkish tone. Their long tail feathers are also darker in proportion. As their name suggests, *violets* have a deep, intense violet color to their body feathers. They, too, have proportionally darker long tail feathers.

Whites of Light Suffusion have white masks and bodies. They also have pure white wings and tails. The primary difference in the white varieties is in the cheek patches, which are a pale shade of the variety they represent.

Whitewings and *Whites of Deep Suffusion (including Skyblue, Cobalt, Mauve, Violet, and Gray)* have white masks that are ornamented on each side of the throat with three gray spots (the paler the better), one of which appears at the base of the cheek patch, which is a pale shade of the variety the bird represents. The general body color of these birds is a very heavily suffused body color approximating to the normal variety. They have pure white wings and tails.

As their name suggests, graywings have gray, rather than black, wing markings. *Graywing Light Green* parakeets have yellow masks with three clearly defined spots of smoky gray on each side of the throat, one of which appears at the base of the cheek patch. Their cheek patches are pale violet, and their bodies are pale grass green. The markings on cheeks, back of head, neck, and wings of graywing light greens should be smoky gray, halfway between black and zero. Their long tail feathers should be smoky gray with a pale bluish tinge. *Graywing Dark Greens* bear a resemblance to the graywing light green described above, but they have light laurel-green body feathers with long tail feathers that are proportionally darker. *Graywing Olive Greens* look like their light green cousins, but the olive greens have light olive-green bodies and proportionally darker tail feathers. *Graywing Gray Greens* have light mustard green bodies, with light gray cheek patches and long tail feathers of deep gray.

Graywing Skyblue parakeets have white masks that are ornamented on each side of the throat with three clearly defined gray spots, one of which appears at the base of the cheek patch. They have light violet cheek patches and clear pale skyblue bodies. Their long tail feathers are grayish blue, and they have pure gray markings on their cheeks, backs of heads, necks, and wings. *Graywing Cobalts* have pale cobalt body color, and their tails have a corresponding color. *Graywing Violets* have pale violet bodies, and their tails have corresponding color. *Graywing Mauves* have pale mauve bodies, with tails of corresponding color. *Graywing Grays* have pale gray bodies and cheek patches. Their tail feathers are deep gray.

The *cinnamon* characteristic we're about to discuss is a sex-linked characteristic that causes the wing markings on a parakeet to be brown, rather than black. Cinnamon birds also have plum-colored eyes, rather than the traditional black eyes. It was first described as "cinnamonwing," but has been shortened to simply cinnamon since it first appeared in 1931.

Cinnamon Light Green parakeets have yellow masks that are ornamented on each side of throat with three clearly defined cinnamon-brown spots, one of which appears at the base of the cheek patch. They have violet cheek patches and pale grass-green bodies. The markings on their cheeks, backs of heads, necks and wings are well-defined cinnamon brown on a yellow background. Their long tail feathers are dark blue with brown quills. *Cinnamon Dark Greens* have light laurel-green bodies, with long tail feathers that are proportionally darker. *Cinnamon Olive Greens* have light olive-green body feathers and long tail feathers that are darker in proportion. *Cinnamon Gray Greens* have pale gray bodies and long tail feathers of a deep cinnamon shade.

Cinnamon Skyblue parakeets have white masks that are ornamented on each side of the throat with three clearly defined cinnamon-brown spots, one of which appears at the base of the cheek patch. They have violet cheek patches and pale skyblue bodies. The markings on their cheeks, backs of heads, necks, and wings are cinnamon brown on white background. Their long tail feathers are blue with brown quills. *Cinnamon Cobalts* have pale cobalt bodies and cobalt long tail feathers with brown quills. *Cinnamon Mauves* have pale mauve bodies and mauve long tail feathers with brown quills. *Cinnamon Grays* have pale gray body feathers and long tail feathers of a deep cinnamon shade. *Cinnamon Violets* have pale violet body feathers and long tail feathers of a pale cinnamon shade. (In all varieties, the male bird carries a deeper shade of cinnamon than the female.) Cinnamon birds also occur in white and yellow.

A gentle spray mist can encourage preening.

Fallow Light Greens have yellow masks that are ornamented on each side of the throat with three clearly defined brown spots, one of which appears at the base of the cheek patch. Their cheek patches are violet, and their general body color is yellowish green. The markings on their cheeks, backs of heads, necks, and wings are dark brown on a yellow ground. Their eyes are clear red or plum, and their long tail feathers are bluish gray. *Fallow Dark Greens* have pale laurel-green bodies, with proportionally darker tail feathers. *Fallow Olive Greens* have pale olive-green bodies and proportionally darker long tail feathers.

Fallow Skyblue parakeets have white masks that are ornamented on each side of throat with three clearly defined brown spots, one of which appears at the base of the cheek patch. Their cheek patches are violet, and their general body color is pale skyblue. The markings on their cheeks, backs of heads, necks, and wings are dark brown on a white ground. They have clear red or plum eyes, and their long tail feathers are bluish gray. *Fallow Cobalts* have warm cobalt body feathers, with long tail feathers that are proportionally darker. *Fallow Mauves* have pale mauve body feathers that have a pinkish tone to them. Their long tail feathers are also proportionally darker. *Fallow Violets* have pale violet bodies and proportionally darker long tail feathers.

Lutino parakeets have an attractive rich yellow color to their body feathers. A lutino's eyes are clear red, its beak is pale yellow, and its legs are pale pink. Adult males have purplish ceres, while adult hens have brown ceres. The long tail feathers and primary flight feathers of the lutino are grayish white. If your parakeet has all of these traits but red eyes, it is a dark-eyed clear if its eyes are plum colored or a yellow if its eyes are black.

Albino parakeets are pure white with pink legs, clear red eyes, and light yellow beaks. Ideally, their feathers should have no blue cast to them at all. White parakeets that have plum-colored eyes are dark-eyed clears, while white parakeets with black eyes are called simply whites.

As their name suggests, yellow wings have yellow (almost melanin-free) wing markings that contrast nicely with the green body color. *Yellow Wing Light Green* parakeets have buttercup masks that are ornamented on each side of throat with three smoky-gray spots (the paler the better), one of which appears at the base of the cheek patch. Their body color is a bright grass-green with buttercup-colored wings and a pale grass-green tail. *Yellow Wing Dark Greens* have laurel-green bodies and proportionally darker long tail feathers. *Yellow Wing Olive Greens* have olive-green bodies and proportionally darker long tail feathers.

Opaline parakeets have less prominent bars on the backs of their heads, and well-marked examples have V-shaped areas on their backs that are free of markings. Opalines also have darker plumage only on their wings; it does not extend from the base of the neck as it does in a normally marked bird. *Opaline Light Greens* have buttercup yellow masks that extend over the backs of their heads and merge into the birds' body color at the butt of wings, which leaves the clear "V" area I mentioned earlier. The opaline's face mask is ornamented by six large black throat spots, the outer two of which are partially covered at the base of violet cheek patches. The opaline light green has a bright grass-green color to its mantle (including the "V" area), back, rump, breast, flanks, and underparts. Its wings should be iridescent and of the same color as its body. Its markings should be normal and symmetrical, and its long tail feathers should not be lighter than its mantle. The *Opaline Dark Green* has a dark laurel-green body. Its long tail feathers are proportionally darker than its body. The *Opaline Olive Green* has an olive-green body color, and it also has proportionally darker long tail feathers. *The Opaline Gray Green* has a dull mustard-green body and gray cheek patches. Its long tail feathers should not be lighter than its mantle. The *Opaline Skyblue* has a skyblue body and suffusion, with a white mask. Like the opaline gray green, its tail feathers should not be lighter than its mantle. *The Opaline Cobalt* has a cobalt body with

Centuries of selective breeding have led to a rainbow of parakeet colors.

proportionally darker long tail feathers proportion. *The Opaline Mauve* has a mauve body and long tail feathers that are proportionally deeper in color. *The Opaline Violet* has an intense violet body. Its long tail feather should not be darker than its mantle. *The Opaline Gray* has a solid gray body and gray cheek patches. Its long tail feather should not be lighter than its mantle.

Yellow Face varieties differ from their normal counterparts in that a yellow-faced bird has a yellow mask, rather than a white one. Yellow-marked tail feathers are also permitted.

Gray parakeets have white masks that are ornamented on each side of throat with three clearly defined black spots, one of which appears at the base of the cheek patch. They have gray cheek patches and a solid gray body color. The markings on their cheeks, backs of heads, necks, and wings are black and well-defined on a white ground. The long tail feathers of these birds are also black.

Spangles, which were first reported in Australia in 1978, show feathering markings similar to those seen in pearl cockatiels. The feathers over the wings are light in the center with dark edgings seen on each feather (including flight and tail feathers). Throat spots also have pale centers.

Lacewings were first reported in 1946. This is a sex-linked characteristic that creates a lacy pattern on the wings of red-eyed budgerigars. These birds also have throat spots and colored cheek patches.

Shedding Some Light on Feather Color

Did you know that light has a lot to do with how colorful bird feathers appear to our eye? Take a hummingbird as an example. These brilliant little winged jewels that flit around our gardens are really quite drab when their feathers are wet and not exposed to sunlight. Refracted light bouncing off tiny ridges on a hummingbird's feathers is what gives these birds their shimmery coloration.

Notice how your bird looks when it takes a bath. Are its feathers as bright as beautiful wet as they are when they are dry? Compare the differences between your bird's wet and dry looks and you'll notice a big difference between them.

Dark-eyed "clear" yellow and *"clear" white* parakeets were first reported in the late 1940s in Europe. They were first described as black-eyed lutino or albino birds, which proved to be an incorrect description, because their eye color is plum rather than black.

Pied parakeets have a combination of colored and clear spots in their feathers. Two types—a dominant and a recessive—are currently bred, and you can tell the difference on sight. Dominant pieds were first bred in Australia in 1935, and they resemble normally marked birds in that they had black eyes and white irises, as well as cheek patches and throat spots. Recessive pieds, which first appeared in Denmark in 1932, have no apparent irises on their plum-colored eyes. They are also more slender than their dominant counterparts.

A lutino Indian ringneck parakeet.

Cresteds, which were first seen in Australia in the 1920s, are available in three forms: the full circular, which has a full "moptop" of feathers; the half circular, which has a crest from a point above the eyes to over the beak; and the tufted, which has a tuft of feathers over its cere. Little interest has been shown to these birds in Australia, and although they remain rare, some are available in the United States and other countries outside Australia. If you are considering keeping cresteds, remember that two crested birds cannot be bred together successfully, because the offspring usually do not survive.

Don't Do It
Never breed two crested parakeets together, because the offspring generally do not survive.

Dusters are unusual-looking birds that crop up occasionally. As their name suggests, these birds look like little feather dusters. They have abnormally long feathers that grow continuously. Dusters are short-lived and unable to fly. The origin of their unusual plumage may be genetic, such as a thyroid or pituitary gland problem.

Red is a color that parakeet breeders are still trying to develop. Some reports have surfaced occasionally of a red or pink parakeet turning up in a breeder's aviary, but these reports have been incorrect or have led to birds that were dyed by their owners. Some breeders have tried crossing parakeets with other small grass parakeets that have red feathers, but so far these attempts have created only sterile offspring.

Black is another color that exists in the realm of the possible where the parakeet color palette is concerned. Like red, though, this color has not yet established itself in aviculture.

Part Three
Beyond the Basics

"Do you take song requests?"

Training Your Bird

What do you think of when someone says, "That's a well-trained parrot"? Does a vision of a macaw riding a bicycle across a high wire in a bird show come to mind? Or perhaps you conjure up a picture of a parakeet reciting complete nursery rhymes. While few people would argue that these are both examples of well-trained parrots, this level of training may be more than a first-time bird owner has the time or patience to achieve initially. Perhaps a more realistic description of a first-time bird owner's well-trained parrot is a bird that can be picked up and handled easily, that doesn't bite or scream excessively, and that may (and I emphasize *may* because there are no guarantees with parrots) learn a few words or simple tricks.

The "step up" command will make training and life simpler.

Canaries and Finches: On Their Own

Although a canary or finch may become tame enough to perch on your finger or eat from your hand, it's probably not worth pursuing advanced training or tricks with these tiny birds. Some hand-raised chicks may become tame enough to tolerate petting, but, in general, canaries and finches would rather not be handled. Therefore, most of this chapter won't apply to owners of these special birds.

So how do you achieve the goal of a well-trained parrot? I have three words for you: practice, practice, practice!

The Ups and Downs of Training

The "up" and "down" commands will go a long way toward helping you maintain control over your parrot. They may be the two most important commands your bird will ever learn to follow because they can be useful in many situations.

To teach your bird the "up" command, have it step onto a stick or onto your hand by gently pressing the stick or your hand up and into the bird's belly while saying "Step up." Your bird will likely step up onto your hand or the stick without much additional encouragement, and it will soon respond to the command without you having to press the stick or your hand into its belly.

As you're teaching the "up" command, teach the "down" command, too. Simply say "Down" as you put the bird on its cage or playgym. These two commands provide you with a great deal of control over your bird because you can use them as discipline methods. They also come in quite handy at the veterinarian's office or groomer as you move your bird from your travel carrier to the examination table or grooming stations.

A Daily Routine

Make training a daily part of your parrot's routine. Not only will this regimen help keep your pet's training up to date, it will also provide exercise for your bird's mind as well as its body. A parrot that has something to do both mentally and physically will be a better-adjusted pet than a bored bird that has little to do to keep its brain and body busy.

Vary the training routine each day to keep things interesting for both you and your pet. Have your bird practice the "up" and "down" commands from its playgym one day, then make it climb a "ladder" you make with your fingers the next. Offer first one index finger, than the other, at slightly higher levels to make your bird climb the "ladder." Keep the sessions short—your parrot has about a 15-minute attention span, and trying to train it for a longer period will only cause both of you to become frustrated. Try to end on a positive note whenever possible, and be positive and upbeat during each session. If you start to become angry or upset with your bird, stop the training session and try it again at another time when you're less tense. Your bird will pick up on your emotions and may start to act up, which will defeat the purpose of the training session.

The location of these training sessions is up to you. Some owners find the training routine to be useful in introducing a bird to a new home. Having the bird perform its familiar routine in unfamiliar surroundings sometimes helps it adjust to the new place more quickly.

You can use unfamiliar surroundings to your advantage if you find your bird is becoming territorial and acting aggressively toward members of your family when it is close to its cage. Take the bird out of the room its cage is in and conduct training sessions in a different room for several days. By taking it to a room it is not attached to, you lessen its need to act in a territorial manner because the bird isn't in its familiar territory.

How To Discipline A Pet Parrot

Many first-time bird owners may be confused as to what method to use to discipline their birds when the

Use treats and praise as encouragement during training.

Going to School

Bird behavior classes are being offered by avian veterinary offices, bird clubs, and even animal shelters. These classes help bird owners better understand their pets' behavior, and they can also help prevent bad habits from forming. Ask for more information about avian behavior classes at your pet supply store or veterinarian's office.

Part 3

birds do something they shouldn't. In the world of avian discipline, some methods are more successful than others.

First of all, remember to discipline, rather than punish, your parrot. Discipline requires that you guide and mold proper behavior, while punishment simply means that you correct a problem behavior, usually by force. Your parrot is a very clever, sensitive creature, and any sort of temperamental outburst on your part will damage the trust your pet has in you. For this reason, it's important to never lose your temper with your bird. You must also never hit it.

Many parrots respond well to what avian behaviorist Sally Blanchard calls "the evil eye." When your bird misbehaves, glare at it sternly and firmly say "No." If the bird is getting into mischief by climbing on or chewing on something forbidden, remove it from the source of temptation as you tell it "No."

Other parrots are sensitive to changes in their owners' voices. My bird was like that. If she was acting up, often all I had to do was say her name sternly or firmly tell her to "Quiet down." By using a stern tone with her when she did not behave as I wanted, I was able to discipline her effectively.

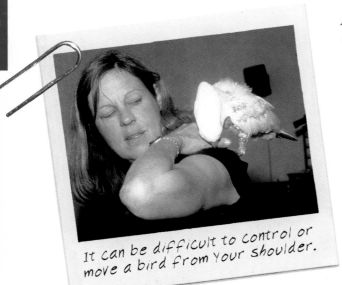

It can be difficult to control or move a bird from your shoulder.

Another discipline method that works well with parrots is to simply ignore them for a few minutes. If your bird misbehaves, put it in its cage and turn your back on it for about five minutes. Ignore it if it screams or otherwise misbehaves in order to get attention. Take it out of its cage when it has settled down and is behaving itself. Because many parrots crave their owners' attention, ignoring them can be an effective way to modify behavior.

In cases of screaming or otherwise agitated behavior, give your bird a "time out" as you would an unruly preschooler. Place your parrot in its cage for a few minutes. Cover the cage to help your pet settle down. Remove the cage cover and let your bird out when it has calmed down.

Over time, you'll learn which methods work best with your bird. Take the time to discipline your parrot properly in the beginning, and you'll be rewarded with a better-behaved bird in the long run.

Tricks To Teach A Parrot

If you have built a good rapport with your parrot and it trusts you, you may be able to teach it some tricks. Some parrots can learn to wave or to roll over, while others can learn to hang upside down from their owner's hand or climb a rope.

To help you determine whether or not your parrot is ready to learn tricks, I'll offer a summary of Kevin Murphy's "tameness scale" that appears fully in his book, *Training Your Parrot*. The farther down the scale your bird is, the more likely it is to be willing to learn tricks.

The parrot will step onto your hand and remain there without jumping off.

The parrot allows you to touch its beak and rub its feet.

The parrot allows you to touch its chest and facial feathers. It will preen contentedly while perched on your hand.

The parrot allows you to ruffle its facial feathers and pet its head.

The parrot allows you to touch its back without protest.

The parrot allows you to pet it under its wings.

The parrot allows you to clip and file its toenails without protest.

The parrot allows you to fully extend one of its wings.

The parrot willingly lies on its back in your hands or on your lap.

The parrot allows you to touch it any way you wish without protest.

Your best hope for trick-training success lies in using and exaggerating behaviors that are already part of your bird's routine. If, for instance, your bird enjoys picking up things with its beak, it may be a good candidate to learn how to drop coins in a bank or to become a slam-dunk star with a bird-size basketball hoop and backboard. If your bird is a chewer, you may be able to devise some sort of parrot card trick that it can do. By learning what your parrot already likes to do and using those behaviors as a foundation on which you'll build its trick routine, you're likely to come up with some clever, unique tricks you and your pet will both enjoy.

My boyfriend's daughter noticed that her parakeet, Andre, liked to follow her around the house, but she worried about his safety around the full-grown and sometimes half-asleep humans in her extended family. To protect Andre from harm, she taught him to stop and look both ways as he leaves rooms and enters hallways to ensure he won't be stepped on. Although she started by placing her hand in front of him and telling him "Stop!" in a firm voice, Andre quickly learned to do what he was told and he rarely goes into the hall between her room and the other bedrooms of our home without checking first for other, larger passersby. He does this trick almost automatically now with little prompting from her.

Simple "tricks" include waving hello or goodbye.

She also taught Andre to pick up and bring her coins that he finds on the table. She has also trained the bird to bring a coin to other people, and he'll drop it in front of whomever she designates. Andre learned this trick as an extension of the normal habit many young birds have of "beaking" or "mouthing" new things in their environment. Because birds don't have hands, they often use their beaks and mouths to explore and test their surroundings. By watching her bird carefully, she was able to turn a normal behavior into a cute trick.

A friend's cockatoo, Gandalf, is a pole-climbing genius, and he shimmies down the legs of his playgym with acrobatic ease. Although this bird hasn't learned a special pole-sliding trick, such a bird could easily become a little "firefighter" answering an alarm or running to hop on a fire truck as it leaves the station. You could condition such a bird to become accustomed to the sound and movement of a toy fire truck by gradually exposing the bird to the light bar's flash and the siren's wail. With patience and persistence, the bird might even learn to ride on the truck itself as an exit after its pole-sliding stunt is concluded.

To condition the bird to the sound and motion of the truck, first show it the truck while the bird is in its cage. Then turn on the truck and let it run through its paces. Judge the bird's reaction—does the truck seem interesting or frightening? Chances are the bird will be intrigued by the lights, the noise, and the motion. Work the truck into the pole-sliding act as you see fit. Perhaps you want to cue the bird to slide down the pole with the siren, or maybe you want the siren to sound after the bird is on the ground. The choice is up to you.

To accustom the bird to riding on the truck, you'll need to start with the basics. Keep the truck near the bird's cage for a few days so the bird can get used to it. Next, place the bird on the back of the truck without the truck being turned on. Let the bird practice sitting on the stationary truck for a few days. Praise it for its perching abilities.

Once the bird is comfortable sitting on the truck, turn the truck on while the bird is aboard. Don't be surprised if your pet hops right off and runs for cover—many birds do. But most of them come right back for more, so don't be discouraged if your pet's first ride is a short one. If there's a way to run the truck without activating the lights and siren, this may be a better introduction to the idea of riding for your bird. Praise your pet when it behaves as you want it to, and gradually increase the amount of time the bird rides on the truck.

Setting Up A Classroom

To start trick training your parrot, you'll need to find a quiet place in your home and gather a few supplies before bringing in your bird for its first lesson. You don't want to be distracted during the lessons, and you want your bird to focus on what you're trying to teach it, so don't try to compete with your child who's practicing for the school music recital or the big-screen TV that your spouse is watching.

In your quiet "classroom," you'll need to have a perch or T-stand on which your bird can sit, a few of its favorite treats (be sure to vary these so your bird won't know what to expect as a reward), and verbal cues or hand signals that you'll use to signal the behaviors you want your bird to learn.

Remember to praise your bird lavishly when it performs a trick correctly. Birds love dramatic tones, gestures, and sounds, so pile on the compliments. Make sure they are sincere because your bird will be able to tell the difference if you aren't. Alternate verbal praise with edible treats as the training progresses so your pet won't become too focused on eating as its reward for a job well done. Be consistent in offering praise and in correcting your pet when it doesn't behave as you want it to. Your bird won't understand a mixed message, so be clear in your directions, praise, and correction.

To get your bird ready to learn, encourage it to do a few "calisthenics" at the start of each lesson. Encourage it to practice the "up" and "down" commands a few times, or have it climb the finger ladder I discussed earlier. Once all the mental cobwebs have been shook out and your bird looks bright-eyed and ready for action, it's time for class to begin!

Now let's discuss some tricks you can teach your pet. We'll look at three simple tricks–waving, nodding, and ladder climbing–and three more advanced tricks–fetching, rolling over and playing basketball.

Beginning Tricks

Waving is a behavior most parrots learn quickly. To teach your bird to wave, have it reach for a pencil with one foot. Hold the pencil just beyond the reach of your bird's foot and say, "Wave." Praise your bird for reaching for the pencil, and make a fuss over the slight lift of a foot at first. Repeat the process until your bird seems to associate the word "wave" with reaching out for the pencil. Eliminate the pencil at this point and prompt your pet with the verbal cue only. Praise and reward good behavior.

Nodding is an extension of a normal parrot behavior, so most birds catch onto it right away. Hold a treat just beyond your bird's beak reach and above its head. Move the treat to directly in front of your bird's beak, then slightly below it so your bird's head moves up and down as it follows the path of the treat. Say "Do you agree?" or some other phrase you'll use as a verbal cue in the future. Reward your bird for "nodding" as it watched you move the treat. Repeat the treat-and-verbal-cue combination and gradually move your hand farther away from your pet. Praise your parrot each time it nods successfully, and eventually phase out the treat. Use the verbal cue to indicate what you want your pet to do and praise it when it performs correctly.

Climbing a ladder may be the easiest trick many birds learn because climbing is such a natural avian behavior. Show your bird the ladder, then place it at the foot of the ladder. If your bird is hesitant to start the climb, place a few treats on some of the rungs for encouragement. Give your bird a verbal cue such as "Go to the top!" as it climbs so it will associate the word and the action. Praise your pet as it progresses up the ladder.

More Advanced Tricks

Fetching is a more complicated trick than it first appears because it involves a multi-step process. In addition to chasing something you throw and bringing it back to you, your parrot must also learn to drop the "fetched" item on cue.

By learning many separate steps, a bird can do more difficult tricks.

Let's break the trick down into its components. A good first step is to teach your parrot to drop an item on cue. Let the bird play with the item you want it to fetch (ideally a small whiffle ball or something that's easy for it to hold in its beak) for a few minutes. When you see it drop the item, say "Drop!" (or whatever your future verbal cue will be) and praise its actions. Repeat this sequence of events until the bird seems to associate the words with the action.

Next comes the actual chasing of the item to be fetched. Toss the item a short distance away from your bird and tell the bird to "Go get it!" Praise it when it chases after the item. Continue this process until the bird seems to understand that the phrase means it will run after this item.

Now comes the final piece of the puzzle: the fetching of the item. For this part of the trick, toss the item away and have your bird chase after it. Tell the bird to "Bring it to me!" and meet the bird as it brings the item to you. Praise it for being such a good fetcher, and gradually extend the training so the bird is praised only when it brings you the item (you don't meet the bird on its return trip after the first few tries) and drops it in front of you on cue.

Playing basketball with a special bird-size hoop and backboard is another multi-step trick. Teach it to your pet by breaking it down into manageable steps, then put the steps together to form the complete trick.

First, show your bird the basketball setup and talk about how fun the game is. Shoot some baskets in front of your bird to demonstrate what you want the bird to do. By being excited about the setup and the trick, your bird will quickly catch your enthusiasm and learn that this new device is something fun!

The next step in teaching your parrot to play basketball is to get it used to the ball. Praise the bird when it picks up the ball, then praise it as it holds the ball for longer periods of time. Using a verbal cue such as "Get the ball!" or "Wanna play?" will help your bird learn to associate your words with its expected action. Use the phrase each time the bird picks up the ball so it will learn the cue more quickly.

One Trick Not To Teach

While there are many cute tricks you can teach your parrot, the one trick you shouldn't teach it is to kiss you on the mouth or preen your teeth or lips. Although this sort of behavior is seen routinely in magazine photos and on pet video shows, it's unsafe for your pet because human saliva contains many bacteria that aren't healthy for a pet bird.

At the same time you're teaching your pet not to kiss your mouth, extend it the same courtesy. If you want to kiss your parrot, kiss it on the top of its head instead. This is safer for both you and your bird!

Teaching your bird to shoot hoops involves a bit of bribery on your part. Hold one of your bird's favorite treats in your hand and show it to your pet. Have the bird pick up the ball, and use the treat to lead your pet to the basket. Reward your pet with the treat when it drops the ball through the hoop. Say "Shoot!" or "Score!" or "Slam Dunk!" as your bird drops the ball in the basket so it will associate the verbal cue with the act.

Combine the ball pickup and basket shooting parts of the trick. Decrease the use of treats and increase the use of verbal cues and praise as your bird begins to master its slam dunk.

Parrot Potty Training

Although some people don't believe it, parrots can be trained so that they don't eliminate on their owners. The trick is as much teaching yourself the clues and cues that indicate your pet needs to eliminate as it is conditioning your pet to associate the act of eliminating with a chosen phrase.

To begin the training process, select a word or phrase that you want your pet to cue to, such as "go potty." Use this phrase whenever you see your bird shifting around or squatting slightly, because these are usually good cues that the bird is about to eliminate. Pay attention to the approximate amount of time between eliminations because you will need to know that in order to avoid any discomfort to your pet later on. Many parrots eliminate about every 20 minutes, so use this as a guide until you learn your bird's personal schedule.

Potty training, though not a necessity, is possible with some birds.

After your bird begins to associate your chosen phrase with the act of eliminating while in its cage or on its playgym, pick it up and hold it until you start to see the body language cues that indicate a need to go. Put the bird back on its playgym or in its cage and say the phrase as it goes. After your bird is through, pick it up and praise it for being such a clever pet! Repeat the process in 20-minute intervals or at whatever interval is required for your bird to eliminate normally. A few accidents are normal as both of you learn this trick, but your efforts will soon be rewarded with a toilet-trained parrot.

How Do I Teach My Bird To Talk?

This is undoubtedly one of the most-asked questions and one of the most popular topics with pet bird owners. The parrot's ability to imitate human speech has fascinated bird owners since ancient times. A Greek doctor named Ctesias wrote about a parrot that could speak Greek and an Indian dialect in 397 BC.

Although no parrot is guaranteed to talk, certain species are well-known for the talking tendencies. Owners of parakeets, African greys, Quaker parakeets, Amazons, and *Psittacula* parakeets have birds that are traditionally good talkers. However, birds from species that aren't known for their talking abilities can develop considerable vocabularies under the right conditions.

Many birds mimic better during face-to-face training.

Too Young to Talk?

Although it's a good idea to start speech training at a young age, that age will likely vary from species to species. For example, parakeets can start speaking between six months and a year, and Amazons can often speak before they are a year old. However, African greys generally don't chat until they are more than a year old.

Tips To Teach Talking

Here are some suggestions that may help you create a feathered chatterbox. All these suggestions assume that your bird is healthy, comfortable, and content in your home:

Take advantage of your bird's normally vocal times during the day and use them for speech training.

Keep sessions short and positive. About 15 minutes is the maximum length the average parrot can focus on training.

Train your bird in a quiet area so it can hear you and you can hear it clearly.

Keep a single pet bird. Birds kept with other birds will tend to learn bird language more readily that they will learn your language.

Limit your bird's access to mirrored toys so it won't form an attachment to its reflection and begin to chatter away to the mirror.

Start speech training when your bird is young.

Begin by teaching one simple phrase, such as the bird's name, and stick with it.

Repeat the phrase to your bird with drama and enthusiasm in your voice.

Speak clearly!

Be patient with your pet. Some parrots do not learn to speak until they are more than one year old.

Use the phrase appropriately each day.

Increase your bird's vocabulary slowly as it learns more words and phrases.

Listen to your pet, especially at bedtime, to find out if it's practicing its vocabulary.

Use talking tapes and CDs sparingly. Some of these recorded media only cause your pet to tune out the phrase you're trying to teach.

Don't be discouraged if your parrot seems to be a slow learner.

If your patient, consistent training shows no results after months of training, your bird may just not be a talker. Most birds aren't. Such was the case with my birds. With my childhood parakeet, my mother tried patiently for a year to teach him to say "Pretty bird." She spoke to him in a bright, enthusiastic tone; she didn't overtax his attention span; she was patient and positive. But the bird remained silent. Years later, she tried to refresh my African grey's memory each holiday season by telling her "Merry Christmas!" in a cheery voice several times a day.

Record-Breaking Birds

Three birds—two parakeets and an African grey—have developed what could be called record-breaking vocabularies. Puck the parakeet holds the Guinness World Record for largest vocabulary by an animal. Puck's vocabulary is estimated at 1,728 words! An African grey named Prudle was reported to have a 1,000-word vocabulary when he retired from public life in 1977.

Sparkie, a British parakeet, was the record-holding talking bird in his time. He won the British Broadcasting Company's Cage Word Contest in 1958 when he recited eight four-line nursery rhymes without a break. At the time of his death in 1962, Sparkie's vocabulary included 531 words and 383 sentences.

Part 3

In both cases, my mother was working with birds with good reputations as talkers. She had birds that were likely to talk, and "Merry Christmas!" had, in fact, been part of my grey's vocabulary with her previous owners. In both cases, though, the birds never learned the phrase she was trying to teach them. To the best of my knowledge, our parakeet never spoke, and my grey's speaking abilities disappeared during her first few years with me. We appreciated both birds for their other wonderful pet qualities and loved them as the special family members they grew to be.

10

Breeding

Because birds are no longer being imported into the United States from the wild, present and future pet birds will have to come from captive-breeding programs. This was not always the case. Until the 1980s, hundreds of thousands of pet parrots (except for parakeets and cockatiels) were captured in the wild and imported into the United States. Many of these birds were less-than-perfect pets because of longstanding health problems or because they had difficulty forming positive relationships with people after they were captured.

When it became apparent that the supply of wild-caught birds would decrease, either through extinction or legislative action, some breeders began to set up pairs of birds as breeders to create chicks

It's hard to resist a baby umbrella cockatoo.

for the pet trade. In many cases, the breeders hand-fed the birds and conditioned them to being around people almost from the moment they hatched.

Because these birds were accustomed to people and were healthier than their wild-caught predecessors, they usually made better pets. Soon, bird owners began to seek out these hand-fed birds over wild-caught specimens. Since 1992, wild-caught birds have not been brought into the United States legally, although smuggling of wild-caught Latin American birds still occurs along the Mexican border.

Breeding Basics

Some people who want to share their love for birds with others do so by becoming bird breeders. Parakeets are popular pets, so we'll use them as an example of how to set up a breeding program.

Mutual preening is a good sign of compatibility in birds.

Other good reasons to choose parakeets include their long history in captivity and their readiness to breed. First-time breeders shouldn't encounter too many problems when breeding parakeets. Here are some suggestions to further ensure success.

Before you actually put your pairs of birds together, ask yourself why you want to breed birds. If done successfully and on a large enough scale, bird breeding can be a full-time job that requires an intense commitment of time and energy. Done poorly, it can bring heartache, headaches, and financial hardship. Done well, it can be a satisfying avocation or vocation.

Start with at least two pairs of mature birds. Parakeets are colony breeders in the wild, and a male parakeet seems to need the noise and competition of another male in the area to stimulate breeding. By waiting until your birds are at least a year old, you will have a better chance for success because the birds' energies will go into breeding, rather than into maturing and breeding at the same time.

Make sure you have a true pair (one male and one female bird). In normal color birds, mature males have blue ceres (the bare patch of skin over the bird's nares or nostrils), while mature females have brownish ceres. Sometimes two birds of the same sex will pair up. If two males pair up, you will see the birds go through the motions of mating, but no eggs will be produced. If two females pair up, they will also go through the motions and lay an abundance of infertile (or clear) eggs that never hatch. In some color mutations, the sexes are difficult to distinguish. If you're in doubt, ask another parakeet breeder or your avian veterinarian to help you determine the gender of your breeding birds.

In the cases of parakeets and a few other species such as Eclectus, determining the gender of male and female birds is a rather simple matter. In most other parrot species, however, males and females look remarkably similar, so other methods of gender determination must be used. These include surgical sexing or DNA sexing. Ask your avian veterinarian for recommendations on which type of testing your birds should undergo prior to breeding.

Make sure your breeding cage is large enough to house both parent birds and a full clutch of chicks (usually three to five) comfortably. Make sure water and food dishes are easily accessible to young birds.

Your breeding birds will need a nest box. If you are breeding your birds in cages, each pair of birds will need a box attached to their cage with a safe hole (no rough edges on the wire, please) cut in the cage wire to allow them access to the box. If you are breeding several pairs of birds in a large flight or aviary, hang more boxes than you have pairs of birds, because invariably two hens will squabble over the same box. By having more boxes than potential parent birds, you reduce the potential for these territorial disputes. Be sure to put the boxes near the roof of the cage or flight because parakeets may not accept nest boxes that are placed low.

The nest box itself is usually made of plywood and measures about 10 inches tall by 6 inches wide by 6

A sturdy nest box will provide sanctuary for both parents.

inches high. The box has an 2-inch-wide entry and exit hole (with a perch the male bird can sit on while feeding the hen so she can feed the chicks) near the top, a movable lid that breeders can open occasionally to check on the chicks, and a small concave niche in the floor for the eggs to rest in without rolling around the box. The concave niche is usually cut into a piece of plywood that slides in and out of the box. Place the niche so that it isn't right in the doorway of the nest box to reduce the chance that your birds may damage their eggs as they enter and exit the box.

Ensure that all perches in the breeding cage are secure. Loose perches can result in infertile eggs because the parakeets are unable to mate successfully on unsure footing.

Breeding birds must be in good health and good condition. Molting birds should not be allowed to breed because the double stress on their bodies may endanger their health. If you have good, healthy birds in top feather, you can introduce the birds to nest boxes and let nature take its course. Some breeders recommend letting the hen become accustomed to the nest box for a few weeks before putting a male bird in the cage with her. Other breeders find success by putting an equal number of male and female birds together in a flight and letting each pair sort itself out.

Nesting supplies for canaries differ from those of parrots.

While you're introducing the birds to each other, you should also be increasing the amount of light the birds are exposed to each day (14 hours is ideal for parakeet breeding) and adding protein to their diets. Offer mineral blocks during this time, too, so the hens can build up their calcium reserves for future eggshells.

About a week after mating, the hen will seem to disappear into the nest box for long periods of time. She is laying her clutch of three to five eggs on an every-other-day schedule. She will incubate them for approximately 18 days. (Note that larger parrot species will incubate their eggs longer than parakeets.) The chicks will hatch in the order their eggs were laid. The parakeet chicks will be blind, naked, and completely dependent upon their parents for survival. Newly hatched parakeets cannot even lift up their heads.

Part 3

Once the hen had laid her eggs, resist the temptation to peek in the nest box frequently. Some hens do not appreciate being checked on constantly, and they may break eggs or kill chicks as a result of the disturbance. Also resist the temptation to "help" a chick out of its eggshell. Chicks need time to absorb nutrients contained in the yolk sac, and they may take up to a day and a half to hatch. This is normal and natural, so don't interfere with the process, or your chicks may not survive.

From their weak and inauspicious beginnings, parakeet chicks gain ground quickly. By Day 6, the chicks' eyes begin to open, followed by the beginning of primary flight feathers on Day 7. By Day 8, a chick can hold its head up, and it begins to take steps around the nest. Tail feathers begin to grow in on Day 9, and the chick has all its down feathers by Day 12. The chicks are the size of their parents by Day 17, can fly at Day 28, have full plumage by Day 38, and are sexually mature by Day 100. (If you are raising larger parrot species, keep in mind that larger chicks take longer to grow, develop, and wean.)

When To Handle Chicks

Chicks that are still in the nest box can be handled, but be aware that some hens do not appreciate nosy breeders and will take action, including killing the chicks, to stop the intrusion. Breeding parakeets do not frequently kill their chicks, but the behavior can become a problem in some of the larger species of parrots.

Parakeet parents become anxious if all the chicks are removed from the nest box at the same time and are kept away from the parent birds for any length of time. This shouldn't discourage you from cleaning the nest box occasionally, but it should encourage you to clean quickly and return the chicks promptly to their parents.

How To Hand-Feed Chicks

Although parakeets are usually such reliable parents that hand-feeding is not needed, occasionally the need will arise. Hens will sometimes reject chicks, or a hen may die suddenly or accidentally. If you do suddenly find yourself with a nestful of chicks to hand-feed, keep two things in mind: heat and cleanliness.

You must strike a delicate balance with the first point, because parakeet chicks must be kept warm, but they should not overheat. Recommended starting points are 85 degrees Fahrenheit for feathered birds and 90 degrees Fahrenheit for unfeathered birds. Adjust the

Hand-fed birds may be more easily tamed than parent-raised.

Don't Do It

Never attempt to hand-feed a chick without some expert instruction. Not only is hand-feeding very time-consuming and tedious, done improperly it can cause serious harm—and even death.

temperature down if the birds start to pant and hold their wings away from their bodies, and adjust up if you see them shivering or huddling together.

Clean hand-feeding supplies and fresh formula will lead to healthier chicks. Keep this in mind if the temptation to cut corners should arise. You should use a different syringe for each baby you feed, and each syringe must be thoroughly cleaned and disinfected between feedings.

To prepare hand-feeding formula, follow the instructions on the package of a good-quality hand-feeding formula. Keep the formula temperature between 100 and 104 degrees Fahrenheit to ensure proper digestion by the chicks. Fill each syringe with the recommended amount of formula (this will vary with the species of bird being fed and the age of the chicks) and place them in a jar of warm, clean water to keep them warm. Get your chicks out of the nest, and place each one in a small, secure container (like an empty margarine tub) with a clean, wadded-up paper towel in the bottom to make cleanup easy.

To hand-feed a chick, put the syringe in the left corner of the bird's mouth and aim the formula in the back right corner of the bird's mouth and throat. Birds have two openings in their throats. The one on the left side is called the trachea. It leads to the lungs. The one on the right side is called the esophagus. It leads to the stomach. You want the food to go down the esophagus and not into the lungs, because it can cause aspiration pneumonia there. Apply firm, gentle pressure to the syringe's plunger and, before you know it, you've hand-fed a bird!

When you are hand-feeding chicks, remember that they are your first priority. Some chicks will require round-the-clock care, and you must be there to provide it.

If you do not want to hand-feed parakeet chicks but you have more chicks than one hen can handle, you might want to consider foster parents. Parakeets generally make good foster parents and do not object to an extra egg or chick in the nest. You can foster eggs or chicks to another pair of parakeets that are on approximately the same egg-laying schedule as your first pair. You can either move unhatched eggs into a foster hen's nest, or you can place recently hatched chicks into a foster hen's nest. Be careful not to overload any one hen, though.

Banding Baby Parakeets

Once your parakeet chicks have hatched and are feeding successfully, you will want to band them. Some states require that parakeets be banded, and serious breeders want their chicks banded to keep track of bloodlines and successful breeding pairs. Also, bird stores may be reluctant to sell unbanded chicks, so if you plan to do business with a store, you will need to have banded your chicks prior to selling them. (Larger parrot species will also need to be banded before you sell the chicks.)

Crop burn is the disastrous result of improper hand-feeding.

You will need to band your chicks when they are about five days old. Some chicks can wait until Day 6, but parakeet chicks grow quickly, which means you have a very small window of opportunity to get the bands on the chicks!

To band a chick, you will need a clean, dry washcloth to set the chick on during banding, a toothpick, a band, and a parakeet chick. (You can order bands from the American Budgerigar Society, from bird specialty stores, or from advertisements in hobbyist publications.)

Place the chick on the washcloth on a tabletop or other sturdy surface, and turn it onto its right side. Hold the chick's left foot in your left hand and slide the band over the two front toes with your right hand. After you've slipped the band over the first two toes, hold the chick's foot with your right hand and continue moving the band up the chick's leg with your left hand, pulling the toes forward and the band back as you go.

The longer back toe may cause a little problem as you pull the band over it. If it does, use the toothpick to flip the band over the longer back toe. The shorter back toe should follow right along (if not, use your trusty toothpick to gently move the band along), and the chick is banded. Reassure the chick that it's a beautiful, brave bird at this point and return it to the nest.

Taking Wing

About four weeks after the parakeet chicks have been banded, they'll begin to try flying. Be prepared to hear lots of flapping coming from your young fliers, but don't be surprised if they try their wings first in their nest box. This will last about a week in most cases, with the first adventurous chick finding its way to the nest box opening for its first look at the outside world at the age of five weeks. Shortly after its first look at the world, this daring young bird will try its first flight. Make sure to have plenty of perching options available close to the nest box opening, because this first flight is traditionally short and weak.

After one chick tests the air, its clutchmates soon follow suit, and breeders are treated to many short, clumsy flights and the chicks' first amusing attempts at perching, side stepping, and turning around on the perches. With practice, though, flying, perching, preening, and other important skills improve. (As mentioned earlier, chicks of larger parrot species will develop more slowly than parakeets, so don't use the parakeet guidelines as a developmental timetable if you're raising a different species of parrot.)

Chicks will hatch in the order the eggs are laid.

Shortly after their first tentative flights into the real world, your parakeet chicks should discover the food and water bowls in their parents' cage. By watching their parents crack seeds, sample fresh foods, and drink water, the chicks should catch on to how to eat, but it will probably take them a week or so to perfect their skills. Breeders will enjoy watching their chicks learning to crack seeds, because the line between foodstuff and toy is sometimes quite blurry for a chick! Like any baby, almost anything a baby parakeet can get into its mouth is fair game. Keep an eye on curious youngsters so that they don't ingest something harmful in these early explorations into the world.

Part 3

Some breeders sell their entire clutches to pet stores en masse, while others prefer a more individualized approach. Talk over your options with the manager of your favorite pet store. Find out if he or she is willing to purchase your birds, and what the conditions of purchase are. You might also want to ask how many birds will the store take at a time, if you can apply the selling price of the parakeets to an account that you can use to purchase supplies from, and the age the parakeets have to be before the store will purchase them.

If you choose to place the babies yourself, you will need to get the word out that you have baby birds for sale. Talk to your avian veterinarian and to other breeders to see if they will help publicize your babies. If your favorite pet store doesn't sell livestock, they might have a bulletin board on which customers can post advertisements of pets for sale. Place ads in your local paper's classified section under "Birds For Sale" and in any animal-themed publications in your area.

Be prepared to do a lot of work on the phone if you place your baby parakeets yourself. You will need to find out exactly what each customer is looking for in a pet bird, and you will also need to gently educate some of them in proper bird ownership. When you do this, try to emphasize the well-being of the bird, rather than the inexperience of the owner.

If callers are hesitant to ask questions, be ready to ask a few of your own. Inquire if the potential parakeet owners have other pets in the home (both present and past). Ask about the person's schedule, how many adults and children are in the home, and if the bird will be a companion for an adult or a child. If you and the caller seem to hit it off, set up an appointment for the person to come see your birds. Be prepared to spend some quality time with each potential owner to ensure that both bird and person get off on the right foot. Some breeders even send along care packages of additional reading material for the owner, familiar food, and a safe, interesting toy to help ease the bird and owner into their new life together.

Breeding Questions
Why does my hen lay eggs out of the nest box?
Inexperienced hens that are bred for the first time may lay eggs outside of the nest box, or a hen may not like the setup inside her nest box. Ideally, the nest box needs to have only a nest block (a piece of wood with a concave niche cut into it that fits inside the box and simulates the bottom of a nesting hole in a tree) and some sawdust. The block keeps the eggs together in the box and the sawdust cushions them.

Should the male parakeet stay in the cage with the female while she sits on the eggs?

Yes. The male serves three purposes during this time: first, he fertilizes the eggs, and then he feeds the female while she incubates the clutch. After the eggs hatch, he feeds the hen so she can feed the chicks. Later on, the male takes over most of the feeding chores so the hen can have a rest.

How many clutches can my birds raise in a year?

Most parakeet breeders allow their parent birds to raise two clutches of chicks a year. Any more than that may overtax the parent birds' health. Larger species may be able to raise two clutches of chicks annually, or you may choose to limit your birds to a single clutch per year.

When is a bird considered too old to breed successfully?

As long as parakeets are in top condition, they can be allowed to breed until they are eight to ten years old. Male parakeets will probably have longer breeding lives than females, because the males do not actually lay the eggs (which is a stressful process for the females) and incubate them. Larger species of parrots mature later and are fertile longer than parakeets.

The tiny beginnings of an African grey parrot.

Why don't my birds' eggs hatch?

Many factors may be at work here, including not having a true pair, having a hen scared off her nest so that the eggs become chilled, contamination from the hen's feces (despite their solid appearance, the eggshells are porous and can allow bacteria in), and incorrect humidity.

How many nest boxes will I need?

Experts recommend that you offer at least as many nest boxes as you have pairs of breeding birds, plus a few extra because hens sometimes squabble over which pair has possession of which box. Usually two additional nest boxes are recommended above the number of pairs that will be breeding.

What's a bonded pair? How do I know if I have one?

Bonded pairs are two birds that enjoy each others' company and have formed a bond that will see them through raising chicks successfully. Bonded pairs often sit next to each other on a perch, preen each other, or feed each other. If your pair isn't bonded, you won't see them spending a lot of time close to one another, and you may notice that they aren't successful at raising chicks.

How many eggs do parrots lay?

The size of the clutch differs between the species. Parakeets normally lay between three and five eggs, while larger species, such as macaws and cockatoos, may limit themselves to a single egg each time they go to nest.

Will my birds use their nest box as a sleeping box?

Again, this depends on the species. Though many other parrot species sleep in their nest boxes, most parakeets use theirs solely for breeding and raising chicks.

My birds laid eggs, but the eggs disappeared before they hatched. What happened?

Some parent birds destroy eggs after laying them. Either the male or the female can be at fault. If you determine that the male is the egg eater, remove him from the cage until the hen finishes laying her eggs, then let him back into the cage so that he can feed the hen while she incubates her clutch. If the female is the culprit, you will have to foster the eggs to other pairs.

To save the eggs in the meantime, you will have to remodel the nest box, drilling a hole in the floor of the nesting concave that is large enough for the eggs to fall safely through onto a floor under the nest box where you can collect them for fostering under more reliable parents. You may also choose to remove the egg-eating birds from your breeding program.

Young parakeets make excellent pets for first-timers.

How old should my birds be before I breed them?

Experts recommend that you let your birds reach at least one year of age before setting them up to breed. By doing this, you ensure that you have a mature pair that can devote its energies to raising chicks rather than two birds that haven't finishing growing themselves. Larger species, such as cockatoos, macaws, and African greys, take several years to mature, so it's best to prevent these birds from breeding until they're several years old.

Do I need to clean or turn the eggs while they're in the nest?

The mother bird will take care of turning the eggs, and in most cases, she will not appreciate any outside help or inquisitive peeping toms around her nest box. Although it's exciting to have a hen on eggs, please don't peek in at your parakeet countless times a day or try to move her off her eggs. Some nosy owners have had their curiosity rewarded by a hen that destroys her eggs, so be careful. A breeder will have to try a daily egg check to see if his or her birds are agreeable to the procedure.

Too Many Eggs

To understand some common breeding problems, let's first look at some vital differences between the avian reproductive system and the mammalian one.

In female mammals, the reproductive system consists of two ovaries and two oviducts (Fallopian tubes), but in birds, the right ovary and oviduct do not develop normally and are nonfunctional.

Female birds can and will lay eggs without the presence of a male bird. These unfertilized, or clear, eggs will never hatch into chicks. If your bird starts laying eggs, leave the clutch with her for the normal incubation time, then discard them. Some birds will lay eggs only occasionally, while others become chronic egg layers.

Chronic egg laying can become a health risk because the hen's body will take calcium from her bones to create eggshells for the developing eggs. If the hen's body runs out of calcium, she runs the risk of laying soft-shelled eggs or becoming egg bound, which means that the eggs do not move along her reproductive tract normally.

An egg-bound hen acts depressed, seems to strain quite a bit, passes scant droppings, and has a bulging vent area. If you notice that your bird shows these signs, take her to your avian veterinarian immediately. Your veterinarian may give your pet injections of vitamins A and D3 or calcium, and he or she may treat your bird with heat, humidity, or injectable hormones.

Be aware that smaller species, such as budgerigars, cockatiels, and lovebirds, seem to be more prone to excessive egg laying, although it can occur in any species of pet bird.

Hens that lay numerous eggs can be treated with hormone injections. If the injections are unsuccessful in stopping the egg-laying process, your veterinarian may recommend that your bird is spayed. This procedure, which removes part of the bird's oviduct, is rather risky and is considered only when other options have been exhausted. Unlike the spay operation that dog and cat owners are familiar with, surgical spaying of pet birds is not recommended under normal circumstances.

Part 3

Fun and Games

This chapter takes you beyond the basics of owning birds. After you've mastered the fundamentals of bird ownership, you may find you want to branch out. Maybe you'd like to know more about some games you can play with your pet. Perhaps you want to take a trip with your bird, or if your bird is an excellent example of its species, bird showing may be in your future. Read on to find out more!

Games You Can Play With Your Bird

Finches and canaries may be less inclined to interact with their owners, but parrots love to play and they love to spend time with their owners, so you can combine the two activities by playing games with your pet. Although these games are designed for

Take time to frolic with your flock.

medium and large parrots, such as Amazons, African greys, cockatoos, and macaws, some of them will work with smaller birds, such as cockatiels and budgerigars. See which ones your bird enjoys playing with you!

Try a bird version of the carnival "shell game" by hiding a treat under a paper nut cup or muffin cup. Your bird will not only enjoy finding the treat, it will also have fun destroying the paper cups along the way. For extra playtime fun, make the treat a nut in its shell so your bird will have to chew and shred the shell in order to get the treat.

Offer your bird a knotty problem to solve by tying several knots in a clean piece of vegetable-tanned leather or rope. Find out how long your bird takes to untie the knots and whether or not it chews through some of them to untie them. Thread raw pasta tubes or cereal "O"s on the leather or rope to add to your bird's enjoyment.

If your parrot seems mechanically inclined, you can entertain it for hours by giving it a clean, large nut and bolt assembly. Go to your local hardware store or home improvement center and find the biggest nut and bolt you think your parrot can comfortably hold and put them together for your pet. A cockatoo I know lets his owners know he's undone the nut and bolt by dropping both into his cage tray with a loud "clang." This is his indication that he wants to continue playing and that his owners need to put the nut and bolt back together so he can have more fun.

Toys and balls entertain a playful rainbow lory.

Keep in mind that birds that know how to undo nuts and bolts probably shouldn't have access to any nuts and bolts that are used to hold up perches in their cages, or that hold the cage itself together. The little feathered mechanic I mentioned earlier unbolted his first cage from the inside out, which caused his owners to marvel at his intelligence and dexterity while pondering how they were going to keep this cockatoo in a cage. A welded-wire cage proved a suitable home for this bird, but it required a keyed padlock to keep the bird safely inside because he quickly mastered the built-in lock on the cage door.

Birds of all sizes enjoy playing "peek-a-boo" with their owners. This used to be one of my bird's favorites. I would loosely drape a beach towel over the top of her cage (with her under it) and wait to see how long it would take her to find her way out. She would squeak and trill and make other happy sounds as she wiggled and chewed and crawled under the towel. She would pop up from under the towel with an excited expression on her face, ready for the fuss she knew I would make over her. (I think she enjoyed that part as much as the game itself.) Be sure to use a towel that's appropriate to your bird's size, and drape it loosely over your pet. Let your bird find its way out from under the towel, and praise and cuddle it when it does.

Another popular bird game is tug-of-war, which you can play by offering your bird one end of an empty paper towel roll (or toilet paper roll, if you have a smaller parrot). Once you've given your end a small tug, the game has begun, and your bird likely won't give up without a fight! Be prepared for a shredded paper towel roll and some spirited competition from your pet. This game can help boost the confidence of an extremely shy bird if the bird is allowed to win regularly.

Because your bird is a clever animal, it may quickly devise its own games. You may discover it enjoys "accidentally" dropping a favorite toy off its playgym so you can pick it up over and over (and over and over) again, or your bird may take pleasure in dangling from its swing by a single toenail to discover how long it takes you to come to its rescue.

Traveling With Your Bird

Some birds see travel as a great adventure, while others prefer to stay home in familiar surroundings. Because your bird probably can't tell you whether or not it enjoys traveling, you will have to do some detective work. Take your bird for a short ride in the car and judge its reaction to the experience. Does it display happy body language, such as hanging on the cage bars and watching the world whiz by the car window, or does it cower on the cage floor and scream?

My parrot loved car rides. She was quite the hit at the drive-up window of local restaurants when I would stop for a quick bite to eat on the way home from the vet's office. Whether it was a short round of errands in the neighborhood or a longer ride to go visit college friends or family several hours away, she was up for the adventure. During the trip, she would nibble on snacks in her cage, play with toys, whistle along with the radio, or carry

Give your bird time to get used to a carrier before a trip.

on what amounted to a conversation with me, offering her vocalizations in response to questions or comments I would make as we rode along.

If your bird doesn't enjoy car rides, you may be able to condition it to tolerate car travel. Although this seems crazy, I know it can work. A friend was able to overcome her cockatoo's car sickness by working with him for more than two months. She determined that his cause of his car sickness was that being in the car scared him, so she started with the basics. She and the bird sat in the car when the car was in the garage to get him used to the car itself. When he appeared comfortable after several days of practice just sitting in the car, she began taking him on short trips around her neighborhood. Over the next three weeks, she gradually lengthened the trips and drove on busier streets. After almost a month of driving on surface streets, she took the bird on trips that included freeway driving. In time, the bird learned to love riding in the car and she soon had company on all her car trips.

As you make your travel plans, one of the most important things to consider is how you'll be getting to your destination. Keep in mind that driving trips with a bird along can be fun for both bird and owner. If you'll be on the road for more than one day, be sure to make reservations at pet-friendly hotels along your route. You can locate pet-friendly motels by picking up a special guidebook at your automobile club office or bookstore. Request a non-smoking room for you and your bird, and clean up any messes completely before you check out.

Air travel with a pet bird requires additional preparation. You'll need to tell the reservations agent that you want to bring your bird along, and you'll need to find out what requirements must be met for a bird to fly by plane. Your bird may be able to accompany you in the cabin in an underseat pet carrier, or it may travel in a pressurized cargo hold.

Part 3

Some of the questions you'll want to ask are what type of pet carrier the airline accepts for shipment, what sort of paperwork is required for the pet to fly, and what the timeframe is for check-in prior to the flight's departure.

After you've figured out how you will get where you're going, the next question to answer is how long you'll be gone. If your trip will take you away from home for only a few days, you and your bird may both find it more enjoyable if a neighbor or friend comes over to care for the bird while you're away. If you'll be away from home for many months, though, you'll probably want your bird to come with you!

If your travels will be taking you outside the United States, it may be best to leave your bird stateside as you travel. Domestic travel with pet birds is far easier for both birds and owners, so seriously consider whether or not you want to take your pet to a foreign country. There may also be restrictions on entering a foreign country with your bird. Research this before you make travel plans.

Once you have your destination in mind and your paperwork in order, the next order of business will be a suitable travel carrier for your pet. If you're traveling by air, you'll have already found out which carriers are airline approved. Here are some tips for selecting a safe travel carrier for your bird:

The carrier must be large enough for the bird to stand normally. It should open easily and be durable enough to protect the bird from harm during the trip.

The carrier should be free of items that could injure the bird during travel.

The carrier should have a grille or subfloor that keeps the bird out of its droppings and other debris that falls to the bottom of the carrier during travel.

The carrier must be well ventilated, and the ventilation holes must have rims on them to prevent the holes from being blocked during the trip.

The carrier should also be clearly marked with your name and destination address. It should also have "LIVE ANIMAL" and directional arrows indicating the upright position of the carrier marked on its side in letters at least 1 inch high.

Part 3

Some birds will play with their owners by lying on their backs.

Options for Stay-at-Home Birds

If you'll be traveling without your bird, you can ensure its care while you're away in a number of different ways. Perhaps you have a friend or family member who can take care of your bird. If that's not an option, you may want to hire a pet-sitter.

Pet Sitters International offers the following recommended quality standards for excellence in pet sitting. Use them as a guide for selecting your pet sitter.

• The sitter is bonded and insured.

• The sitter provides references.

• The sitter has experience in caring for pets and is clearly mindful of their safety and well-being.

• The sitter provides written literature describing services and stating fees.

• The sitter visits the client's home before the first pet sitting assignment to meet the pets and get detailed information about their care.

• The sitter shows a positive attitude during the initial meeting and seems comfortable and competent dealing with animals.

• The sitter wants to learn as much as possible about the animals in his or her care.

• The sitter provides a service contract that specifies services and fees.

• The sitter is courteous, interested, and well informed.

• The sitter takes precautions to make sure a client's absence from home is not detected because of any careless actions or disclosures by the sitter.

Part 3

Part 3

• The sitter conducts business with honesty and integrity and observes all federal, state, and local laws pertaining to business operations and animal care.

• The sitter has a veterinarian on call for emergency services.

• The sitter has a contingency plan for pet care in case of inclement weather or personal illness.

• The sitting service provides initial and ongoing training for its sitters.

• The sitting service screens applicants for employment carefully.

• The sitter calls to confirm or has the client call to confirm the client has returned home as scheduled.

• The sitter refrains from criticizing competitors.

• The sitter provides a service rating form for clients.

• The sitter exhibits courtesy and professionalism in all dealings with staff members, customers, and industry colleagues so as to present the pet sitter and the pet sitting industry favorably and positively.

• The sitter keeps regular office hours and answers clients inquiries and complaints promptly.

Another option to consider is boarding your bird at your avian veterinarian's office. Ask a member of the office staff for more information about boarding procedures for your pet. Spaces fill quickly during busy travel times, so make your bird's reservations early to ensure it will have a place to stay while you're away!

Travel Carriers

Good	Not Good
Acrylic carrier	Paper bag
Wire-fronted hard-sided carrier	Cardboard box
Soft-sided carrier	Pillowcase
Wooden carry box	Owner's bare hands

Certain birds, such as this gouldian finch, are naturally showy.

Traveling To See Birds

Some bird owners just can't get enough of parrots and other bird species. They not only keep pet birds in their homes, they also include bird parks, zoos, and aviaries in their vacation plans. Others take birding trips within the United States or to other countries to watch birds in their native habitats.

I admit it, I'm one of these people. In addition to sharing my home with a parrot for more than ten years, I never pass up an opportunity to go see birds when I'm on vacation. I catch bird shows at zoos and theme parks, shoot rolls of film of the birds on display at different attractions, and make conversation with other bird lovers I meet in my travels. I haven't traveled abroad to see birds yet, but I have seen wonderful collections at aviaries, zoos, and theme parks around the United States.

When I worked at *Bird Talk* magazine, I was fortunate enough to get some behind-the-scenes tours of breeding facilities, zoos, and aviaries that only added to my appreciation for and fascination with parrots. Similar tours are available at zoos and theme parks for a nominal fee. Contact attractions in your area to find out if you can take part in behind-the-scenes tours. If you're traveling out of state, ask your travel agent to find out about special tour opportunities at attractions you plan to visit. If you're making your own travel arrangements, study guide books, brochures, and websites to locate these extra activities–they're well worth it!

Showing Your Bird

Although not yet as popular as dog, cat, or horse shows, bird shows offer owners and breeders a chance to show off

You can interact with many different birds in zoos and theme parks.

their pets, as well as chance for bird lovers to meet and talk about one of their favorite subjects: their birds. Bird clubs sponsor shows around the country. Some are small, while some attract entries from across the country. In all cases, they are a fun and enjoyable way to learn more about different types of birds.

In a show, birds are judged against a written standard of what an ideal representative of the birds' species is. This ideal bird doesn't yet exist, but breeders continue to strive toward that perfect written standard when breeding their show birds. For birds entered in the Society of Parrot Breeders and Exhibitors-sanctioned shows, the standard is divided into five categories: conformation (40 points), condition (30 points), deportment (15 points), color (10 points), and presentation (5 points). Birds are compared against other birds of the same species to determine the winning entries in the show.

Joining a bird club is the first step most new exhibitors take on the road to show success. In many cases, experienced breeders or exhibitors are also part of the club, and they can provide tips to newcomers who are willing to learn about bird showing. The show season usually takes place in the fall, which is when breeders usually don't have as many breeding pairs on eggs. This means they can devote some time and energy to showing some of their birds.

Before you show your own birds, go to some shows to get a feel for how the judging process works. You can also find out which birds are winning, and you can meet the breeders of these birds after judging has concluded and ask if they have any birds for sale.

When you have birds with showing potential, you'll need to begin training them for the show routine. A good show bird is the picture of health, from its bright eyes to its perfect feathers to its clean feet. It is calm during judging. It acts interested in its surroundings and is not alarmed when strangers approach its cage to judge it.

In many cases, birds are shown in special show

Bird shows can be a good way to see a variety of birds.

cages. Dimensions and cage color information can be found in the show catalog. Ask your fellow bird club members if your bird will need a special cage to participate in shows.

If your bird will need a show cage, it will need to become adjusted to that cage before it takes part in its first show. Start your bird's exposure to its show cage by setting the show cage close to the bird's regular cage. Leave the show cage door open and allow your bird to explore it during its supervised out-of-cage time. You want your bird to sit calmly on its perch in the show cage, so praise your pet whenever it sits on the perch for an extended period of time.

After your bird has become comfortable perching in its show cage, ask some friends over and have a practice bird show. Get one of your friends to act as a judge. Have the judge look the bird over closely while standing next to the cage. Also ask the judge to tap the cage bars lightly and gently poke at your bird with a pencil or pointer in order to get the bird used to the judging procedure. Reward your bird's good behavior by praising it.

While you are training your bird to conform to show behavior, you must also begin to groom it for the show circuit. As mentioned earlier, a show bird must have all its feathers in perfect condition. (This means it cannot have clipped wings.) A show bird also needs trimmed nails and clean feet. Consider your bird's molting cycle when planning to enter a

Rules for Bird Show Exhibitors

- Arrive on time.
- Maintain a positive attitude at all times during the show.
- Follow all posted signs.
- Be quiet during judging so that you don't indicate in any way that the bird being judged is yours.
- Remember that all judges' decisions are final.
- Don't complain about any decisions to members of the show staff or to other exhibitors because that may make you look like a poor sport.
- Treat show staff members with courtesy and respect.
- Compliment show staff members when they do a good job.

show. Some exhibitors don't show birds that are molting, while others believe it can be good practice for both bird and exhibitor. Discuss this topic with other bird club members to find out what's worked for them.

Once your birds have become comfortable with the show routine, try entering them in some local shows. Obtain a catalog from the show committee and study it carefully. It is a valuable guide to what's going on at the show, so be sure you know all the details.

Review the catalog carefully when you get it. Make sure to double-check your bird's check-in time because late entries are accepted at the discretion of the show committee. Also look at the entry fees and payment methods so you won't be embarrassed by bringing your credit card to a show that accepts only checks or cash. Finally, check to see when your birds will be judged and who will be doing the judging.

The catalog will also provide you with information about the divisions, subdivisions, sections, and classes that will be judged. Read this part of the catalog closely because it's information you will need as you fill out your bird's entry forms. Birds can be disqualified for incorrect forms, so review your forms carefully before you hand them in.

The show judges are looking for a perfect bird during judging, so less-than-perfect birds shouldn't be entered in competition. If your bird isn't in tiptop condition, don't enter it in the show.

When show day arrives, be sure to arrive at the show hall in plenty of time to fill out your paperwork. Turn in your forms and your bird to the registration desk, then walk around the show hall or commercial exhibit area to see the other birds being shown or the product displays. Pay attention to the time because you don't want to miss your bird's appearance before the judges.

As your bird is being judged, don't do anything that would indicate to other members of the audience that it's your bird being evaluated. Be a gracious winner and an even more gracious loser. Don't dispute a judge's decision or start an argument. Congratulate the winners, and be positive and courteous at all times. At the end of the show, collect your bird promptly from the show committee. Compliment committee members on a job well done and head home to plan your strategy for the next show!

Resources

Periodicals

AFA Watchbird
American Federation of Aviculture, Inc.
P.O. Box 56218
Phoenix, AZ 85079-6218
602-484-0931
www.afa.birds.org

Bird Talk
Subscription Dept.
P.O. Box 57347
Boulder, CO 80323
www.animalnetwork.com

Bird Times
Pet Publishing, Inc.
7-L Dundas Circle
Greensboro, NC 27407
www.birdtimes.com

Birds USA
P.O. Box 6050
Mission Viejo, CA 92690

Companion Parrot Quarterly
2236 Mariner Square Drive, No. 35
Alameda, CA 94501
510-523-5303
www.companionparrot.com

Veterinary and Aviculture Groups

American Federation of Aviculture
P.O. Box 56218
Phoenix, AZ 85079-6218
602-484-0931
www.afa.birds.org

Association of Avian Veterinarians
P.O. Box 811720
Boca Raton, FL 33481
561-393-8901
www.aav.org

National Animal Poison Control Center/ASPCA
888-426-4435
www.napcc.aspa.org

Conservation, Research, and Rescue Groups

Avicultural Society of America
P.O. Box 5516
Riverside, CA 92517-5517

The Gabriel Foundation
P.O. Box 11477
Aspen, CO 81612
www.thegabrielfoundation.org

International Aviculturists Society
P.O. Box 2232
La Belle, FL 33975

Midwest Avian Research Expo (MARE)
10430 Dewhurst Rd.
Elyria, OH 440335
www.mare-expo.org

Society of Parrot Breeders and Exhibitors
P.O. Box 369
Groton, MA 01450

U.S. World Parrot Trust
P.O. Box 341141
Memphis, TN 38184

World Parrot Trust
Glanmor House
Hayle, Cornwall TR27 4HY
England

World Parrot Trust Canada
P.O. Box 29
Mount Hope, Ontario LOR 1WO
Canada

Bird Clubs and Societies

African Lovebird Society
P.O. Box 142
San Marcos, CA 92079-0142
www.africanlovebirdsociety.com

African Parrot Society
P.O. Box 204
Clarinda, IA 51632-2731

Amazona Society
P.O. Box 73547
Puyallup, WA 98373

American Budgerigar Society
1704 Kangaroo
Killeen, TX 76541

American Canary Fanciers Association
2020 Kew Dr.
Los Angeles, CA 90046

American Cockatiel Society
P.O. Box 609
Fruitland Park, FL 34731

Asiatic Parrot Association
734 S. Boulder Hwy., Suite 400
Henderson, NV 89015

Bird Clubs of America
P.O. Box 2005
Yorktown, VA 23692

Cockatoo Society
26961 N. Broadway
Escondido, CA 92026

Fig Parrot Group
8023 17th N.E.
Seattle, WA 98115

Forpus Fanciers
P.O. Box 804
Jamul, CA 92035

International Loriinae Society
P.O. Box 4763
Plant City, FL 33564-4763

International Parrotlet Society
P.O. Box 2428
Santa Cruz, CA 95063-2428

Macaw Society of America
P.O. Box 90037
Burton, MI 48509

North American Parrot Society
P.O. Box 404
Salem, OH 44460

National Cockatiel Society
286 Broad St., Suite 140
Manchester, CT 06040

National Finch and Softbill Society
P.O. Box 3232
Ballwin, MO 63022

Parrot Rehabilitation Society
P.O. Box 620213
San Diego, CA 92102-0213
www.parrotsociety.org

Parrot Society of Australia
P.O. Box 75
Salisbury, Qld 4107
Australia

Index

Photo Credits

About the Author

Julie Rach edited *Bird Talk* magazine from 1992 to 1995. She has written seven books and numerous magazine and online articles about bird care. She had a budgerigar when she was a child and owned an African grey parrot with a variety of physical and emotional problems for more than ten years. She and her boyfriend live in Oceanside, California, where his daughter keeps two budgerigars.